Indie Author's Toolbox

How to create, publish, and market your kindle book

Copyright © 2014 / 2016 by Nick Vulich

Contact me at

- E-mail: hi@nickvulich.com
- Blog: indieauthorstoolbox.com

Amazon Author Page:

- amazon.com/author/nickvulich
- amazon.com/author/nicholasvulich

Table of Contents

Why you need to read this book 1
The times they are a changing...4
Getting started 7
Help! I can't think of anything to write about 8
Choosing a topic to write about 11
    List your book on Kindle..18
    Reports – Community – KDP Select 24
    Establish Your Author Presence on Amazon 26
    Amazon Book Optimization 39
On Amazon Promotions..53
    KDP Free Days 56
    Using Kindle Countdown Deals...59
    Kindle Unlimited 64
Off Amazon Promotions 66
    Social Media..68
    Reviving a dead book..71
Publishing beyond Amazon 76
    Create Space 78
    Audible (ACX)...86
    Babelcube 91

    Smashwords 96

    Draft2Digital 101

    Barnes & Noble 104

    Kobo 108

    Lulu 112

    Google Play & Google Books 117

Final Wrap up 122

Read these books next 124

Been there, done that 130

    Interview with Steve Scott..**132**

    Interview with Buck Flogging 138

    Interview with Martin Crosbie 147

    Interview with Rob Parnell 154

About the Author 161

Books by Nick Vulich...**163**

Why you need to read this book

Thousands of new Kindle books are being released every day. If you want your books to keep selling, you need to keep them fresh and up to date.

I'm surprised at how many bestselling books never get updated. Six months, or a year ago, when the author first released them, they offered the latest, most up to date information available, and all the reviews reflected that. But now – the reviews say something entirely different. "It's out of date information. I tried what the author said, and it wouldn't work. Don't waste your time or money."

Let me give you an example. Just over two years ago Kindle gurus cracked the Amazon HTML code. Dozens of books were written proclaiming this one small trick could help you sell thousands of extra books. Six months ago Amazon started to send out notices they were going to enforce HTML standards, and listings that violated their policies would be taken down.

What this means is no more pictures in book descriptions. No more videos.

Ninety-five percent of these books have never been updated to reflect the new policies. Why? The authors don't care enough about their books to keep them current.

It's not just the little guys who don't update their books. I recently downloaded a copy of *Ninja Book Marketing Strategies* by Tom Corson-Knowles. His first chapter discusses book page conversions. He talks about adding a tracking link in an image, and then explains how to use Amazon's special HTML code. (Only problem is, authors haven't been able to use that code for six months.)

The reason I singled Tom's book out here is in the introduction to his book he makes a point of talking about how he takes special pride in keeping his books up-to-date and current. He explains that he just spent a boat load of time updating one of his social media books so it contained the latest info available. Hmm! He probably should have updated this book before putting it up for a Countdown Deal.

Let me give you another example. These same eBook gurus suggested writing reviews in your genre was a great marketing tool to bring readers to your books. To make it work, you just had to change your profile name to "author a. author, author of my greatest book," (or in my case—Nick Vulich, author of *History Bytes*). It was a great strategy, and it worked for over a year. Then one morning I woke up and discovered Amazon had changed my signature to "An Amazon Reader" for all of my reviews. Once again, very few authors have updated their books to reflect this change.

Why is this so important?

Other authors are watching.

You have to keep an eye out for interlopers in your niche. It's like a jungle out there. These are the new guys. They smell the money you're making. They can't wait to grab a piece of your action. Who can blame them?

You don't have to worry about most of them. These guys are lazy. They copy and paste, taking a little from here, and a little from there. It's mainly bullshit, and no one's going to read their books anyway. But there are a few really smart poachers out there. They study what you're doing. They focus in on a segment of your niche looking for a spot where they can grab a foothold, and they run with it – adding book after book to their catalog.

You need to intervene early.

Smart authors constantly study their niche, and their competition. Look at your niche the way one of these interlopers would. Ask yourself, what else is there? Can I get more specific? Rather than write about selling on eBay, can I write about selling clothes on eBay? What areas do my readers need to know more about – international shipping, lowering fees, bookkeeping, etc.

Be proactive. Go after those niches before the trolls push you out of your own market.

Add new information every six months, every year at the least. Write a bold headline, and place it at the top of your book description – new and revised on 09/09/15. This lets everyone know your book is current and up-to-date.

Authors Note: This is just one of the many invaluable tips you will find packed between the covers of this book.

Let's get started.

The times they are a changing

Looking back on it **TV** may have played too big of a part in my childhood. Every memory I have revolves around some sixties or seventies TV series.

I turned five in 1963. The Beatles made their debut on the *Ed Sullivan Show*. Later that year we watched JFK get his brains blown out on live TV. For years after that I remember watching reruns of his horse drawn casket being pulled down Pennsylvania Avenue.

By the mid-sixties we were riveted to the TV set as "Uncle Walter" Cronkite brought us the war live from Vietnam. War correspondents droned on about guerilla fighting, I read a comic book that showed oversized gorillas carrying machine guns and bazookas through the jungles. Dumbass that I was, I thought they were real fricking monkeys slugging it out over there.

1966 brought us *the Monkees*. Adam West debuted as *Batman*. He danced the Batusi, had a way cool ride – the Bat Mobile, and whenever he laid hands on the bad guys, they flashed those really cool signs—Bam! Ka-Pow! Owie!

In 1969 Neal Armstrong walked on the moon. That's "one small step for man, one large step for mankind." We traveled halfway across the country in the back of a station wagon, visiting Vegas and California. All I remember is we didn't have air conditioning. When you rolled down the windows in the Painted Desert hot air lapped your face like a sick dog.

In 1970 a friend of mine swallowed a really strange purple pill. Jughead jumped out of an *Archie* comic book and talked to him. What the f*#k!

That same year National Guard troops blasted the hell out of thirteen kids at Kent State, killing four of them. Four years later a bunch of self-righteous journalists chased Richard Nixon out of the White House for lying.

I left home in 1976 for this thing we called college. The pungent odor of Mary Jane drifted through the halls of the English Philosophy Building at the University of Iowa. No one gave a second look as teaching assistants smoked pot with their office doors thrown wide open.

One of the Philosophy TA's, "Bear Grease," would perch himself on the table in front of us. He was like a chimney puffing smoke and words between each draught on his cigarette. By the time class wrapped up fifteen to twenty smoking missiles stood straight up around the edge of the table.

I met Jane Fonda, and her husband, Tom Hayden, when he was campaigning for president. Gus Hall, the communist party candidate, provided comedy relief at another political rally. The rest of that time was a blur of failed dreams, the original *Saturday Night Live*, and enough booze to drown a fish. I saw Jefferson Starship, the Grass Roots, Charlie Daniels, Linda Ronstadt, and Steppenwolf.

Sometime in the late seventies I took an American literature class taught by David Morrell. The only thing most of us could think about was this is the guy who wrote *Rambo*. Walt Howerton, an aspiring poet taught rhetoric, and I learned to "howl" like Alan Ginsberg.

In between all of that I wrote a lot of crazy ass short stories. So many of them one of my writing instructors asked me if I could even write normal, rather than all of this convoluted shit I was turning in. I think I wrote a fifteen page paper on the presidential elections just to quiet his ass.

Next thing I knew it was 1980, and I had to grow up. No more partying. No more writing. I had to do this crazy thing called make a living. I got a haircut, bought a suit, and became one of them.

And, then it's 2012. I got a whack on my backside, my head, I don't know, but I wrote my first book, *Freaking Idiots Guide to Selling on eBay*.

And, everything changed.

If Kindle had been around in 1976 I'd have probably published a thousand books by now. Instead, I lost the 32 years between the time I graduated from college in 1980 and 2012 when I discovered my writing self again.

The things I could have told you by now.

I've got a lot of years to make up for so let's get started…

Getting started

Are you having trouble picking the topic for your book? Maybe you've finished writing your book, but you've got questions about the mechanics of listing it on Amazon – How do you write a compelling description? How do you know you've got the right cover? What are key words anyway, and why do they matter?

Have you just published a new book to the Kindle store, and found yourself wondering what's next?

You aren't alone.

Publishing your first book, or even your tenth book on Kindle is a daunting task. As an Indie author you're going it alone, or with limited help, and that means everything about your book is left up to you. You need to choose a topic that's going to sell; write a compelling story that keeps readers flipping the pages; make sure it's edited properly – typo free, formatted for a variety of Kindle devices and other e-readers. And, then, there's the matter of creating book covers, writing descriptions, choosing keywords, and let's not forget about getting reviews.

Being an Indie Author can be scary at times. That's what this book is all about, helping you through the maze of publishing your book and getting it discovered on Kindle.

Help! I can't think of anything to write about

Do you ever wonder where people pick up crazy ideas? You know what I'm talking about - the man on the moon, the canals of Mars, and little green men from outer space.

Back in the late 1890's to early 1900's there was an amateur astronomer named Percival Lowell. He read the works of Camille Flammarion and Giovanni Schiaparelli, and became convinced there was life on Mars. Most guys would've read a book or two on the subject and let it go at that. Lowell had some extra money jingling around in his pocket and built a full-fledged astronomical observatory to support his obsession.

He searched out the perfect location for it which just happened to be on a hill outside of Flagstaff, Arizona. He named the spot Mars Hill, and over time it developed into the world's largest private observatory.

Over the years Lowell penned three books: *Mars*, 1895; *Mars and Its Canals*, 1906; and *Mars as the Abode of Life*, 1908. He mapped out a whole series of canals crisscrossing the planet. Not satisfied with that Lowell developed a theory about an entire civilization forced to the point of extinction on their dying planet.

He rushed to get his observatory completed before 1894. That was when the two planets would draw closest together, and he expected to enjoy a front row seat for the upcoming Martian invasion.

When the impending invasion didn't materialize Lowell continued his studies. He gave lectures and spread his message about the strange civilization he had discovered on Mars.

The scientific world vehemently disagreed, arguing Lowell was deranged, or at the very least his observations were half-baked. Other astronomers couldn't see the canals. "The atmosphere was too thin to support life," they said. "There's not enough gravity."

None of these criticisms deterred Lowell. He responded the reason they couldn't see the elaborate system of canals was the ability to see them depended upon atmospheric conditions. They happened to be just right when viewed from his observatory. Life on Mars was different he argued. The rules of gravity and atmosphere that existed on Earth didn't apply to beings from Mars.

Lowell continued his astronomical studies until his death in 1916. When he died he endowed his observatory with a tidy sum of money, and entrusted them to find what he called the missing planet – "Planet X."

In 1930 "Planet X" known today as Pluto was discovered by the team at the Lowell Observatory located on Mars Hill.

What does all this have to do with writing?

As writers each of us creates entirely new worlds in our heads. We cling stubbornly to them adding facts, sometimes changing the laws of physics, or commonsense to support our creations.

In a way we're no different than scientist. We start with a hypothesis (or a simple question) ... we ask ourselves what if the world is square, or what would the world be like if Hitler won World War II, or why do good things have to be so bad for us?

Sometimes we know the worlds we're creating contradict the laws of commonsense and physics, but that's half the fun of it.

When you're writing about something you've got to make it so real, you and everyone else, just has to believe it, no matter what!

How else can you explain Hobbits and such?

Or if you really can't think of anything to write about, you may just want to take a gander back through history and study the works of misunderstood geniuses like Percival Lowell.

Choosing a topic to write about

Choosing a topic to write about is part art, and part science.

Good ideas for stories are all around you, but finding one that will sell is another story altogether. If you write nonfiction there are three topics that are always in demand – health, wealth, and love. Fiction can be broken down into fads – chick lit, vampires, and zombies.

The great thing about Amazon is it's easy to become a bestseller in your category.

Here's why.

According to the book *Bestgorize* by Joe Oye, Amazon has 3847 categories, and when you dig deep down into each category, they number the top 100 bestsellers in each category.

If you want to be a bestseller, this gives you 384,700 opportunities.

Think about that for a moment. Most authors are never going to write a number one bestseller, or even make the top 100 bestseller list on all of Amazon. There's too much competition for those spots, and for a lot of authors the subject matter of their book further limits these opportunities.

But, with a great book, and a thorough understanding of how the Amazon market place works, just about anyone can publish a top ten bestseller in their category – Maybe even a number one bestseller

The even better news is – You don't have to write a number one bestseller to pay the bills. Authors can make a decent living on Amazon publishing books that rank in the top ten or twenty books in their category.

Here are six techniques to help you research book topics using Amazon.

1. Look over books on Amazon's bestseller lists.
2. Read book descriptions for books that are similar to what you want to write.
3. Use the "Look Inside" feature to read the first few chapters of books similar to what you're considering writing.
4. Check out book reviews to discover what people like and don't like about given books.
5. Look over the table of contents so you better understand what your competitor's books are about.
6. Read the highlights. At the bottom of the book description page Kindle shows the top highlights for each book. These are the sections people plan on coming back to. If you don't do anything else, read the highlights to discover what readers think is important.

Let's take a look at each of these topics in more detail.

Check out competing books on Amazon's bestseller lists.

This one should be a no brainer. If you want to write a bestselling book, you need to understand what is currently selling.

First off, take a quick look through the top 100 overall books on the Kindle marketplace. Be sure you are looking at paid books. You want to make money, and these are the books readers are shelling out real cash for. Amazon also lets you search in the free store. Just keep in mind, there's a big difference between what people are willing to pay for, and what they will gobble up for free.

The first thing you're going to discover is fiction outsells nonfiction. Fiction and nonfiction directed towards women outsells books written for men. A recent study by *ComScore* noted that 56.6% of *Kindle* owners are women. Another survey conducted by *Bowker* in 2011 found that women purchase three times as many books as men. What does that tell you? If you want to sell more books, you need to choose topics that grab women by the seat of the pants, and make them want to buy your book.

As you're looking at titles on the bestseller lists zero in on categories that interest you. Pay close attention to the top forty books in each category. Most readers won't look past the first page or two of results when they search for a book to read.

When you search for topics to write about, you want to find categories with a number of books ranked under 30,000. The top one or two books in the category should ideally rank under 20,000. No book in the top ten should rank over 50,000.

What these numbers tell you is there's a chance you might be able to make some money. A book ranked under 10,000 sells around 20 copies per day. A book ranked at 20,00 sells around 7 to 10 copies per day, and a book ranked at 50,000 sells roughly 2 or 3 copiess a day. If your book is priced at $2.99 this gives you an opportunity to make $200 to $1200 per month based on sales.

If the majority of bestsellers in a category rank 100,000 or higher you probably want to rethink your book idea. Even if you have something really special to say, it's going to be a tough sell.

Read descriptions of books similar to yours. What does the author have to say about the book? What benefits will the reader get from reading it? Does the description talk about the contents? Does it focus on learning a new skill? Does it keep you entertained? Is the approach humorous? Educational? Or serious?

You need to get a feel for the book, and the author's approach to the topic. This will help you narrow down your focus so you can distinguish your book from others that have already been published.

Take a moment to look at the book description for *Farthest North: America's First Arctic Hero and His Horrible, Wonderful Voyage of the Frozen Top of the World.* The description builds suspense by outlining the situation the members of the Advance were in, how the entire world assumed the crew was dead in the Arctic cold, and how Captain Elisha Kent Kane remained undaunted by the tragedies he faced.

The entire story is set up in four short paragraphs. It is followed by a quick introduction to the author, a list of his previous books, followed up by two glowing reviews.

It's a great description, and makes you want to read more. If you're an author who wants to write about a similar topic you quickly learn exactly what you're up against.

Use the "Look Inside" feature to see what your competitor's books are all about. As you're looking at books and trying to develop a topic, use the "Look Inside" feature to learn more about the books you discover.

Pay special attention to the Introduction or Why You Need to Read This Book section. This will tell you what topics the author feels are special about his book. Often times authors of nonfiction books will lay out the steps, or the methods, they're going to follow to solve a problem.

As you read the first few chapters, study the content. Make notes about what subjects it covers. Pay close attention to the author's tone. Is it conversational, like he's talking to a friend? Is it boastful, helpful, or more authoritative?

The tone a book is written in is just as important as what the author has to say. If the book is boastful, reviews will often reflect this, and say "all the author could talk about was himself." If the author writes in an authoritative tone, many times the reviewers will say his style is "condescending," or that "he talks way over your head."

Pay attention to the writing style, and tone of other books in the category. Use that information to help craft the proper voice for your story.

Read reviews for books similar to yours. What do people like about the book? What don't they like? Most reviewers say what they wish the book would have been about, or what information they wish would have been included in the book. Use these reviews to develop a better and more complete book. When you write your book description, or why you need to read this book section, be sure to let readers know your book includes information mentioned in the reviews.

Study your competitor reviews. If there are enough of them they will tell you exactly what to write.

One of the books that comes to mind here is *Zealot: The Life and Times of Jesus of Nazareth* by Reza Asian. The book has 3,000 reviews. Over ten percent of them are one star. If you take time to read the one star reviews they're loaded with detailed comments. There are comments on why the book is wrong; where its thesis is flawed; and what the author should have talked about, or used as evidence.

You could easily write a dozen or more books just by reading through the negative comments on this book. The reviewers give you everything you need to know to write a follow-up bestseller.

Read the table of contents. The table of contents can be a goldmine of information for authors. A quick glance through it will show you what content is included in the book; details about how to organize your topic; and what topics the author decided weren't important enough to include.

A lot of times when I page through the table of contents, I get ideas for new books. One book I read about selling on eBay had a short chapter on selling books that just barely scratched the surface of what's involved. After giving it a little thought, it turned into one of my latest books – *How to Make Money Selling Old Books and Magazines on eBay*. A couple years ago I read a book about social media that briefly mentioned the new *Twitter Vine App*. Those three paragraphs morphed into my book – Twitter Vine App Explained.

If you know enough about your topic, a quick look at the table of contents will reveal information the author chose not to include. Use these points as ammunition to add value to your book. Or if you take exception to conclusions the author makes, take a moment to explain why you disagree with what the experts have to say, and why you think your idea is better. This will help distinguish your book from the competition.

If you're not sure how to do this I recommend *They Say / I Say: The Moves That Matter in Persuasive Writing* by Gerald Graff and Cindy Birkenstein. It is geared more towards grad students, and explains how to frame arguments for academic papers, but the information is just as valuable for everyday writers. Consider it a whack on the side of the head to get your creative juices flowing. The ideas contained in this one book may just spawn a bunch of book ideas for you.

Michael Alevar used this contrarian strategy to construct the title of his book – *Make a Killing on Kindle (Without Blogging, Facebook, or Twitter)*. Just about every book written about self-publishing up to that point said you had to blog, comment on Facebook, and Twitter, and connect with readers wherever possible, or your book wouldn't sell. Alevar's book boldly challenged that theory.

Read the book highlights. Kindle displays the top highlights at the bottom of each book description page. Readers only highlight text they feel is important, or they want to come back to. Kindle makes highlights more relevant by telling you how many readers highlighted each comment.

If you want to do quick research on a Kindle book, scan through the contents, and read the highlights first. This will tell you the key takeaways readers thought were important. If 200 readers highlight several sections on eBay listing descriptions, or 150 readers highlight a section on how to use the Send to Kindle App you can assume these are topics readers would like to know more about.

Make a note of the important highlights, and be sure to include content about them in your book. Consider turning some of the highlighted content into a stand-alone book or guide. If 200 or more readers took the time to highlight a particular section, it's a good indicator there is a strong interest in the topic.

List your book on Kindle

Before you list your book on Kindle you need to set up your account. Go to https://kdp.amazon.com/.

If you already have an Amazon account you can sign in with it. Otherwise choose sign up and follow the directions provided. They're quick and painless.

After you sign into your KDP account you should see four headers across the top of the page: Bookshelf, Reports, Community, and KDP Select. To get started with your book scroll part way down the page until you see add new title. Click on it, and you will be ready to set up your Kindle book.

Publishing your book to Kindle is pretty self-explanatory. If you ever find yourself in need of help click on the blue <why?> link by each step, and Amazon will explain more about what you need to do.

The blue box at the top of the screen gives you the opportunity to enroll in KDP Select. KDP Select lets authors make their book available for free to Kindle readers for five days in every 90 day period. Amazon Prime members are allowed to borrow one free book every month. By enrolling in KDP Select your book is made available to these readers. Each time your book is borrowed through the Kindle Lenders Library you receive a piece of the KDP Select fund set aside for authors. The current payout is averaging approximately .0058 cents per page read. In exchange for enrolling your book in the program, you are required to make your book exclusive to Amazon for ninety days.

The next two sections ask you to provide your book title and subtitle. If your book is part of a series put a check in the next box, and enter your series title. When you do this Amazon will tie all of the books in a series together and include the series title along with your book title in search results. Edition number is optional. Most times I will type in first edition, and update this for any subsequent revisions I make to the book. If you're self-published most often you don't have a publisher so you can leave the publisher line blank. If you established your own imprint to sell your books you can add the publisher name here.

You have 4,000 characters to describe your book. That works out to somewhere between 600 to 800 words. I cover descriptions in more detail in the section titled Amazon Book Optimization. The least you need to know is your description needs to entice readers to buy your book. Give them a compelling reason to click on the buy button.

You can dress your book description up using HTML. Here are some of the HTML codes Amazon currently supports.

. <b> bold </b>

.
 creates a line break or space. To leave a blank space between lines you would use the code twice

. <h1> to <h6> to create bold headings. Most commonly you will use <h1> to create a large headline. *(Many books still suggest <h2> creates the large bold headline in Amazon orange, but that capability was removed during early summer of 2015.)*

. <hr> _____ </hr> creates a rule to divide sections of your description

. <i> formats your text in italic </i>

. <li> creates a list. You would use <ol> around each item to create a numbered list </ol>. To make a list set off with bullet points you would use <ul> </ul>

To see the entire list of HTML code supported in Amazon book descriptions click on the following link https://kdp.amazon.com/help?topicId=A377RPHW6ZG4D8

When you are format your description using HTML, every command needs an opening and closing code. For example <b> begins formatting the text in bold. To stop formatting text in bold you need to close the code with the following line </b>. Using the / in the brackets tells it to stop formatting in that style.

Book contributors lets you enter the author, co-author, illustrator, editor, etc. The default language is English if you are publishing in the United States. Change it if necessary. Publication date will fill in automatically, so you can leave it blank. If you revise your book you can fill in the date so your book shows a more recent publication date. Many readers purchase books with more current publication dates because they expect them to have the most up-to-date information.

Where it asks for an ISBN most often you will leave this blank and Amazon will supply a book identifier for you. If you purchased an ISBN you can enter it here.

During step 2 you are asked to verify publishing rights. If your book is in the public domain (meaning it is out of copyright, or has no copyright) select this option. If you hold the copyright to your book, select this is not a public domain work.

FYI: if you're publishing a public domain work it is not eligible to be enrolled in KDP Select.

Step 3 helps you target customers for your book. The first step is to add categories. Amazon has 3847 categories to choose from. When you list your book you are allowed to select two categories. Click on add categories and select those that best match your book. Over time Amazon will slot your book in the categories it feels best fit your book.

The next section lets you add seven search words or keywords to help readers find your book. I cover how to locate keywords more in the section on Amazon Book Optimization. The very least you need to know is - keywords are terms readers use to search for your book on Amazon. Don't include your title or your name, Amazon will already search by these. You are also not allowed to include other book titles or author names. Doing this violates Amazon's Terms of Service and can get your account suspended. If you want readers to know you write like Steven King, or your book is reminiscent of Forrest Gump, mention it in your book description, not here.

Some self-publishing experts say you should use "Kindle Unlimited" as a keyword to target free seekers. Don't do it! It's a violation of Amazon's TCs, and eventually they will make you change it, or take your book down.

Section 4 is where you upload your cover, or create a cover using Amazon's cover creator. To upload a cover file from your computer select browse for image to locate the file.

Section 5 lets you upload your book file. Before you can upload your book file you need to select your DRM (Digital Rights Management) settings. These determine whether readers will be able to copy and loan files of your book after they purchase it. The only stipulation is that once your book has been published you cannot change the DRM settings.

Section 6 allows you to preview your book. When you select this you can see what your published book will look like on the Kindle Fire, iPad, and iPhone. **FYI**: A manuscript that looks perfect in word, can take on an entirely different look on an e-reader. Make sure to look at every page using the previewer. Look for page breaks, extra lines, pages not displaying the entire text, gaps in the text where you have several extra lines, and anything else out of the ordinary. This gives you the opportunity to correct the most common formatting errors before you press the publish button.

There's also a box just below this labeled download previewer. I always use the Send to Kindle App to read my book on my Kindle

Fire, and iPhone. When you read the book the way the majority of your readers will it makes it easier to catch errors and correct them.

After you've completed these steps, select Save and Continue, to move to the next page, and finish setting up your book. Or, if you're not ready to move to the next section, select Save as Draft, to save all of your information for later.

Section 7 verifies your publishing rights. Most times authors will select worldwide rights, but if you only hold publishing rights in certain territories select individual territories, and choose the ones that apply.

Section 8 is where you select your royalties. If the selling price of your book is less than $2.99, or over $9.99 you should select the 35% royalty option. If the selling price of your book is between $2.99 and $9.99 you should select the 70% royalty. After you select the royalty rate you need to enter your list price. When you enter the list price it shows you your royalty rate, delivery charge, and estimated royalty.

FYI: If you selected the 70% royalty rate Amazon charges you a delivery fee based on the size of your file. The larger your file the higher your delivery charge. (If you're worried about delivery charges keep the pictures, illustrations, and charts in your book to a minimum. Be sure to compress all of your files before embedding them in your manuscript.)

You can mark the checkbox to have all of your prices based on the United States price, or you can set the prices for individual territories separately. The fine print below the pricing section explains how the VAT tax will be applied in Europe and Great Britain.

Section 9 lets you enroll your book in the Kindle MatchBook program. MatchBook allows readers who purchased the paperback version of your book receive the eBook for free, or at a discounted price. The nice thing here is even if you set your MatchBook price to 99¢, Amazon will pay you the 70 percent royalty rate.

Step 10 enrolls your book in Kindle Book Lending. This lets book buyers lend their book to a friend or family member for fourteen days one time. By default, all books making a 70% royalty are enrolled in the lending program. You can opt out of the lending program if your book is earning a 35% royalty.

After you've completed entering all of the required information, you need to accept Amazon's terms and conditions. Then select save and publish. Your book will be available for sale in the Kindle store within twelve to forty-eight hours, usually sooner.

Anytime you want to make changes to your book you can come back to your Bookshelf and make changes.

Reports – Community – KDP Select

This is where you track sales and earnings for your Kindle titles. Amazon recently revamped the reports section.

Sales Dashboard. Kindle authors can finally track their earnings in dollars, Euros, Pounds, etc. Before this revision authors knew how many units were sold, but were never certain what that meant in dollars and cents so this revision is a welcome change. You also have a graph to show you unit sales, borrows, and free titles over a variable period of time.

Promotions lets you track the progress of your Countdown Deals. The nice thing is they show you how many sales you made during the promo, what your royalties are, and then compare promotional sales and revenues to those in the previous period. As a result it's easy to determine how well your Countdown Deal performed.

Month-to-Date Unit Sales. This is the old dashboard most Kindle authors are familiar with. It shows you your daily sales by title.

Prior Month's Royalties shows you how much money you made for a given month. Normally the reports are available after the fifteen of the next month.

Payments. Payments lets you track deposits Amazon makes to your bank account. Beginning about the 20th of the month Amazon begins emailing notices a payment is being processed for your account. Most often payments are deposited in your bank account on the 30th of the month. There have been a few months

I've been pleasantly surprised and found my royalties deposited in my account between the 23rd and 25th.

The community tab is basically a forum where you can ask other Kindle authors questions, or you can jump in and answer questions for them.

The KDP Select tab explains the KDP Select program in more detail and gives you a spot to enroll your books.

Establish Your Author Presence on Amazon

Amazon created **Author Central** as an area for writer's to showcase information about themselves and their books.

One thing we know: If people like your book they're going to want to know more about you. What you look like; how you got started writing; where you live; and what other books you've published.

To claim your Author Central page, visit the following link:

https://authorcentral.amazon.com/gp/home?ie=UTF8&pn=irid37437482

Upload an author biography to introduce yourself. Add a picture so readers can have a look at your bright and smiling face. Author Central gives you a place to collect all of your books in one place so readers can browse through them. Each time you publish a new book, be sure to click on Add Book, to add your latest title to your list of books.

Another interesting option Amazon offers is the ability to link your blog and Twitter account to your Author Central Account. When you do this your most recent tweet shows up, along with highlights from your three most recent blog posts.

You can upload book trailers or promotional videos. If you're photogenic, or good with video, you could create a whole series of videos to let readers learn more about you and your books.

Many writers link their books to their Facebook fan page or their author website, but a link to Author Central might pay off better over the long haul. Not only does it introduce readers to you, it gives you a great opportunity to sell more of your books.

This section is going to explore Author Central in more detail, and help you set up a profile that sells you, and your books.

Claim your books

The major advantage of using Author Central is it gives you a spot to collect all of your books in one location where fans can easily find them.

To claim your books click on the Books tab in the Author Central banner. This will bring up a page that shows Books by your name. Below this you will see a yellow button that says Add more books. Click on it, and paste in the ISBN number of your book. If you don't have it handy, you can type in your name or the title of your book and search for it that way.

When Amazon shows your book, confirm that it is your title and it will be added to your list of books.

Every time you publish a new book, or add a new version (paperback / audio book / Kindle) make sure to add it, to make it easier for readers to locate your book.

Author Bio

Your author bio gives you another chance to sell yourself and your books.

How you write your author bio depends upon the type of books you write. Match your bio to your writing style. If you write humorous books, comedies, or satire make your bio light and breezy. If you write authority books on specialized topics, use your bio to position yourself as an expert in your field. Talk about your advanced degrees, years of experience in your field, awards, and other publications.

A lot of novelist talk about themselves, their family, their pets, or what inspired them to write.

The key is to make your author bio unique and informative. Think of it as your elevator pitch. Answer these questions – Who are you? What do you do? How can readers benefit from reading your books?

How to write a great author bio

As authors we're always trying to promote ourselves, and do what we can to put our works in front of a new group of readers.

The problem is a lot of authors take the shotgun approach. They blast their message out to everyone, hoping a few people will act on it. It's possible one or two readers may take a peek, and maybe even drop $2.99 to buy your book, but the odds are it's going to miss its mark with most of the people you broadcast your message to.

The thing is you're casting too wide of a net. When you target everyone you're likely to miss the folks who would be most interested in purchasing your book. I think Sean Platt and Johnny B. Truant put it best in *Write. Publish. Repeat.* They say to tell your story. Go into detail about who you're writing for. Tell readers who your book is, and isn't for, and don't worry about turning away a bunch of potential readers. You're better off finding your true followers. Over the long haul it's going to save you a lot of grief, and negative reviews, from readers who aren't a good match for your message or your writing style.

What you need to do is develop a brand statement. You should to be able to sum up what you're all about in one sentence.

In my case, I write short easy to implement solutions designed to help readers overcome ecommerce problems related to selling online – specifically on eBay, Amazon, Etsy, and Fiverr. That's a good start at my brand statement. Overtime I've narrowed it down even further. I wanted to make it as easy as possible for readers to understand what I'm all about.

Here's what I finally came up with –

Short easy to read solutions to your ecommerce problems.

That's my entire brand statement. Nine easy words tell readers all they need to know to decide if I'm the guy they're looking for or not.

How about you? Can you sum up your brand in less than ten words? If not, you need to take a really good look at what you're doing, because if you can't easily define yourself, neither can potential readers.

When you define your brand this way it's going to do one other thing for your writing. It's going to keep you focused on what's important to your readers. In my case, each of my books needs to be short, easy to understand, and focus on solving one particular ecommerce problem. If each book does that I fulfill the promise I made to my readers.

My brand statement is the opening line to my author biography for most of my ecommerce books. After it I add a sentence or two to flesh it out so readers can get a little better idea of what my books are all about.

Here's the long version.

Short easy to read solutions to your ecommerce problems.

Most of my books can be read in under an hour. The information in them can be put to work immediately to help you sell more products on eBay and Amazon, services on Fiverr, or eBooks and books an Amazon and Kindle.

Let me ask you again. What is your short and long brand statement?

Write it out. Incorporate it into your author bio. It will sell a lot of books for you.

Profile picture

I think I'd rather go to the dentist and have a tooth pulled than have my picture taken, but the fact is – readers want to see your picture. They want to know what you look like. They want to know you're a real person.

A simple thing like posting your picture on Amazon Author Central can help you sell more books.

It's crazy, but true.

Look at other author pictures in your genre. If they're all suited up, you probably should be too. If they're dressed in business casual go with that. A lot of authors like to pose with their kids, or their dog. That's okay too, especially if you write fiction. If you write about business, or more serious topics, wear the suit.

Sports writers can get away with wearing a team jersey. Diet and exercise gurus would look best in shorts or sweats.

One other suggestion, pay someone to take the background out of the picture. Just include your figure, it looks more professional.

Tailor your author picture to what you write.

Add your Twitter feed & recent blog posts

Another great way to build your brand is to link your Twitter feed, and most recent blog posts, to your Amazon Author page. When you do this your, Amazon Author page will display your most recent Tweet, and your three most recent blog posts.

To add your blog or Twitter feed, go to Author Central. Choose add multimedia, blog feeds, a Twitter feed. Click where it says Author Central Profile. Towards the bottom of the page you will see a section labeled blogs. Click at the top where it says add blog.

What you're going to paste into this link is the RSS feed from your blog, not your blog URL. If your blog is hosted on Blogger, scroll down to the bottom of your blog where it says Subscribe to Posts. When you click on this it will display a bunch of code in your browser window. Ignore that and go up to your browser address bar. Highlight the URL, copy and paste it into the box in Author Central.

If you use WordPress to host your blog the location of your RSS feed is going to depend upon the template you use. After you locate the correct link do the same thing. Click on the Subscribe to Post option or RSS Feed. Paste the URL from the browser address bar into the box on your Amazon Author page.

Adding your Twitter feed is much easier. After you add your blog, you will see a column labeled Twitter. It's over to the far right side of the page. Click where it says edit account. This will bring up a box asking you to type in your Twitter username. Once you've done this, your most recent Tweet will appear to the right of your author bio. Be patient. It can take a few days for your blog posts and tweets to begin displaying.

Add events

The events section lets you add speaker engagements, book signings, and conferences, or other events you are scheduled to attend.

When you fill in this section you make it easier for fans to connect with you in person. It also reinforces your authority platform, and helps to position you as an expert. When readers see you are a featured speaker at conferences, writer's workshops, or similar events, they assume you are an acknowledged expert in your field.

Add photos and videos

These two sections let you add a visual element to your profile. I added my picture, and a number of my book covers. I've seen authors upload several different pictures of themselves, their pets, or their families. Others display pictures that complement their books. Look at what other authors in your category are doing. Upload the pictures you feel best represent your brand.

People love videos. There's no question about that.

I had Professor Hans Von Puppet of Fiverr fame make a video promoting one of my books. I also had a white board video promoting several of my books, so I uploaded them to YouTube, and linked them to Author Central.

Some authors record a welcome video talking to readers about their books. Other authors make elaborate video trailers for their books and upload them here. Like photos, videos are a personal preference. Experiment with different types of videos, and see what works best for you.

If you have the patience, and know how to make them, a series of short how-to videos (2 to 5 minutes long) would make a great lead in to your books.

You could also have someone conduct a short interview with you about one of your books, why you write, or even about a charity close to your heart. Choose something that draws readers into your story.

Author Central can even help you spy on your competition. Really? They have a section that shows readers other authors who write books similar to yours.

If you're not sure who your competition is check it out. Bookmark these authors. Read their books. Study their book descriptions, and author bio. Hell! You may even want to buy a few of their books from time to time and see what they have to say. It could open up an entirely new world of possibilities for you. It could be you will discover a hole in their catalog that lets you jump in and add a new title.

While you're checking out your competition here's another idea that should help you sell more books.

Recently, a number of authors have teamed up to promote their books. What they do is drop their book prices to 99¢ for a day, or for a weekend. They take a group shot of the book covers, and each author posts about the special on their blog or website. To supercharge things even more, they mention it on Facebook, and Tweet about the promotion. The few authors I've seen do this have built some good momentum, and sent their books skyrocketing up the charts.

What about you?

It's easy to get started. Email other authors who write in your genre or a similar category. Tell them you'd be interested in running a promotion with them and several other authors. Explain how it could benefit all of you by allowing you to reach a larger audience by piggybacking off of each-others followers.

Not convinced, or need some more ideas to make it work?

. Horror writers could promote a spooktacular around Halloween or Friday the 13th.

. Romance writers could offer a Valentine's love fest

. History writers could promote a plethora of books focused on President's Day, the Fourth of July, or Thanksgiving.

No matter what genre you write in there's a holiday, or something special going on that you can promote around. Strap on your thinking cap, dream up new ideas, and sell more books.

Reports, Reviews, and More

Author Central also keeps you up-to-date on your author rankings, and recent reviews.

When you look at the blue tab at the top of the page you see six headings – Home, Books, Profile, Sales Info, Rank, Customer Reviews, and Help.

Home is a quick overview. It shows you links to other Amazon sites – Audible, Create Space, and Kindle Direct Publishing. It also contains links to update your profile and book lists.

Books gives you the opportunity to add books to your bibliography. Select add books and follow the prompts.

This section also lets you add more content to your Amazon book description page. I want to take some time here to describe each of these sections in more detail, because they give you an opportunity to really grab your reader's attention, and sell more books.

To get started click on the book you want to update. This will take you to the book's page. In the upper right corner you will see a list of the different formats the book is available in – Paperback, Hardback, Kindle, Audible, and any other editions. You need to add content to each of them individually, so if your book is available in three formats, you would need to go into each one of them and post the information separately. At this time you can't add information for audio books (hopefully Amazon will change this soon).

When you click on the Books tab three sections are shown – Editorial Reviews, Book Details, and Book Extras.

Editorial Reviews lets you add extra content to your book's description page. A few of these sections don't apply to eBooks specifically. I'm going cover their intended use, and then I'll give you a few ideas on how you can make the most of them to help you sell more books.

Reviews. The best use for this section is to highlight your top three of four reviews. Don't post the whole review. Pick out one or two key sentences. Emphasize key points in italic, list the authors name in bold below it.

Product description. You can post your book description here, or in KDP when you upload your book. If you use bold titles or Amazon orange (no longer available) in your descriptions don't list them here. Once you've posted your description in Author Central you can't update your descriptions using KDP anymore.

From the author. You can talk about yourself, talk about your book, or take a few moments to introduce the subject matter of your book. I posted a self-interview in this section for all of my eBay books. It gave me the opportunity to tell readers why they should sell on eBay, and how to get started. **FYI**: This is prime real estate. What you post here is going to display on your book description page just below the customers who bought this item also bought section. Make every word you put here count.

From the inside flap. This section was designed for traditionally published books. The information on the inside flap is supposed to go here. eBooks don't have an inside flap so it's an opportunity to get a little creative. I use it to talk about the changing nature of eBay, and how my books can help you to sell more in this volatile climate.

From the back cover. Once again, this section was designed for traditionally published books to list the information from the back flap. As an eBook author you need to use it to your advantage. Too many eBay books promise readers they can become a millionaire overnight working five hours a week. I let potential readers know up front it doesn't work this way. You can make a decent living selling on eBay, but it takes a lot of hard work. This distinguishes me from the get rich quick scammers and con artists out there.

About the author. Normally your author bio from Author Central displays on your book description page. For some books you may want to use a different version of your bio. That's where this section can come in handy. I write on a number of different e-commerce topics. When I write about job search I include a different bio that focuses on how I help clients in their career search. When I write about social media, my author bio reflects my expertise in that area.

I've read a lot of books that suggest you shouldn't bother filling in the above sections. They say it is information overload, and it's just going to confuse readers. These are the same guys who say you should keep your book description short. Their thought is your book description shouldn't be longer than two or three paragraphs. My thought is that's a waste of prime real estate. You need to tell more to sell more.

It's true. Most readers are just going to scan through your book description, or added sections, looking for information that interests them. There are also a lot of readers out there who hang on every word, and check out every detail before they make a purchase – even if it's a 99¢ eBook.

The key takeaway from all this is to be creative. Use the different sections to include information that will help sell your book. Include short excerpts. Profile your main characters. If your book is set in a foreign country or strange locale, talk about the customs there.

Have fun with it.

Switch it up a little. Change the information you include on your book description page from time to time. Market researchers say most people need to be exposed to an advertising message at least eight times before they make the decision to purchase a product. Give them something different to look at each time they come back to your book description page.

Book details is something you can't change. It lists the publisher, date of publication, number of pages, and such.

Book extras applies more to fiction. You add the content here using Shelfari.

You can discuss your top three characters. Give a simple outline of your plot. Add quotations from your book. For science fiction and fantasy you can add a glossary of words and terms to help readers of your book. There's also a section where you can add any awards your book has won.

Keep in mind you don't have to add any of this content. It's extra information that can help sell your book. If you're uncomfortable getting started you can baby-step it. Add one section today and another in a few weeks or months when you're ready.

The Sales Info tab lets authors keep track of how their books are selling in paperback and hardback editions. The sales are recorded by Book Scan and are updated on your page every Friday. If you read through the information on how it works, they tell you which sales are included in the numbers, and which aren't. The info tab says only 75% of your book sales are actually reported, and that sounds about right to me. All of my books are published through Create Space and the numbers don't match up with Book Scan, probably because expanded distribution numbers aren't reported by Amazon until two or three months later after the distributor pays for them.

Rank lets you know your author standing on all of Amazon. You can get a snapshot of how your sales rank for all books (paperback, hardback, and Kindle), Kindle only, or books (paperback and hardback).

You can also dig down into categories for your individual ranking in each category you write in. Use this tool to track your growth in a category. Each time you add a new book it should nudge your ranking up a notch or two.

Customer reviews is just what it says. Reviews normally show up here two or three days after they're posted on Amazon. It's an easier way to read them than constantly checking your book page. This section gives you the option to comment on book reviews, however, I wouldn't recommend doing that. Some authors like to say thank you for good reviews. Some authors get caught up commenting on bad reviews. Nothing good can come from this. The best strategy is to read your reviews. Take what you can from them, and move on.

The Help tab explains in more detail how to use Author Central. If you have any questions it will answer most of them for you.

Amazon Book Optimization

Psst! Do you wanna know a secret?

There are no secrets. No tricks. No magical incantations you can invoke to sell more books on Amazon, or any other online book site for that matter.

Selling more books is all about how you manage the basics.

It's about —

1) Writing a good book

2) Selecting a killer title

3) Creating an attention grabbing cover

4) Writing a book description that compels readers to click the buy button

5) Choosing keywords that drive searchers to your book

6) Ensuring your "look inside" sample sells your book

If you perform these six steps well your book is going to sell. Misfire on any of them, and you're likely to have problems.

Just so you know, some of the advice I'm going to give you here goes contrary to what you're going to get from most of the "experts." In my four years of indie publishing, I've taken a lot of wrong turns. I've been fed a lot of bad advice. All I can tell you is what has worked best for me. The best advice I can give you is to experiment often. Don't be afraid to try new things. Keep the ones that work, discard the ones that don't. Keep building your bag of tricks, and over time you'll develop a system that'll work for you.

With that said, let's dig deeper into each step and see how you can use them to position your book for success.

Write a good book. Abraham Lincoln said it best, "You can fool all the people some of the time, and some of the people all the time, but you cannot fool all the people all the time."

If you don't have a good book, the reviews are going to catch up to you, and people are going to stop buying your book. Sure. You can sell a few copies of a bad book. Sometimes you can sell a whole lot of copies, but eventually the reviews are going to sink your career.

There are a lot of Kindle advice writers that tell aspiring authors you don't have to write well. Don't waste too much time editing your work. Just do the best you can, and get your book out there. Sell a few copies, and then write your next book.

Last year, or the year before, that advice might have worked. But readers are getting smarter. They've downloaded a lot of worthless crap over the past few years, and they're tired of it. If you don't believe me, read the reviews. Most readers are honest, and they call it like they see it. If you're book smells like a load of horse hockey, they're going to say it. If enough readers jump on the band wagon, there's no going back.

Forget the books that tell you how to write a book before breakfast, over your lunch break, or on a roll of toilet paper while you're sitting on the throne. At the same time, forget the books that tell you you can write a book in seven days, twenty-one days, or even thirty days. The fact is you can write a book in the time it takes you, no more, and no less.

There appears to be a fundamental disconnect between what readers want, and what some writers think readers want. Many writers believe readers want to read short books. The majority of reviewers say just the opposite – here are a few of the reviews major novelists recently received for their Kindle Shorts.

. A throw away sixty pages. Lee Child

. Don't waste time and money buying the ads, wait for the book itself. Janet Evanovich

. It's so short it isn't even a short story. Dean Koontz.

. Good writing for the beginning of a novel, with no real ending. Steven King

No matter what anyone tells you, most readers don't like short. It makes them feel like they missed out on something, or that the writer was just out to take their money. Consider this the next time you go to publish a short manuscript.

The key to selling more books is to write a complete book that leaves readers feeling satisfied. If you can do this, you're golden. You will get enthusiastic reviews. Readers will tell their friends about you. They will race out to buy your book the day it's released.

Select a killer title. Too many writers try to stuff a load of keywords into their title hoping they can game the system. Search engines may find keyword bloated titles enticing, but real readers are turned off by titles too big to fit on the book cover.

They can't remember them. They don't understand them. They don't know what to think about books that use them.

Short is better. One to three words is the perfect length for a title. It's easy to remember. There's very little chance for confusion. As a result, you're going to sell more books.

Check out the following five titles. They're short. They're memorable. They do a good job of revealing what the book is about. And, if I didn't mention it, they're selling a lot of books.

. *Story $elling* by Nick Nanton & J. W. Dicks

. *eBay Seller Secrets* by Ann Eckhart

. *Declutter your Inbox* by S. J. Scott

. *Killing Jesus* by Bill O'Reilly

. *Email Marketing Blueprint* by Steve Scott

Compare that to these titles.

. *7 Steps to Sales Scripts for B2B Appointment Setting* by Scott Channell

. *How I Make Money Every Day Automatically When Others Sell on eBay* by Xavier Zimms

. *Author's Quick Guide to Making Money with your 99¢ Kindle Books* by Kristen Eckstein

. *How to Write and Publish your Book on Amazon and on Kindle* by Eldes Saullo

. *How to Write a Kindle Book that People Want to Buy before Breakfast* by James Bedford

Use your main keyword in your title. Use a combination of two or three keywords. Don't string together a series of two or three keyword phrases in your title. It doesn't make sense.

Instead, write a short title. Follow it up with an awesome subtitle that tells readers a little more about the subject matter of your book. Once again, keep the subtitle short. Less than ten words are best. Include your most relevant keywords in your title and subtitle. Place your other search terms where they belong – in your book tags, and in your description.

Make your cover sizzle. Readers are going to be attracted to your book by three things – the title, the cover, and the buzz surrounding it.

Whatever you do, don't design your cover yourself. No matter how good you think you are, or how great you think your idea is, don't design your own cover. Don't let your best friend, or baby sister do it either. Your cover is too important to be left to chance.

I gotta admit I'm a serial Fiverr. I've outsourced 179 graphic design gigs on Fiverr in the last six months. Some of the work you receive is so-so, but a lot of the gigs posted on Fiverr deliver professional quality designs. The results, like anything else, depend upon the effort you put into it.

I use rroxx for most of my covers. He does great work, and my projects are always delivered on time. Here's the link to his gig if you want to check it out.

http://www.fiverr.com/rroxx/create-awesome-professional-ebook-cover-design.

You can also outsource your cover on Elance, 99 Designs, or odesk. Each of these sites has experienced graphic designers who can help you design a professional cover to help sell your book.

The best way to get a great deign is to know what you want before you select a designer. Look at other books in your genre. You don't want to steal someone else's design, but normally there's a common theme running through many of the book covers in a genre. If you find something you like, download it, and send it to your designer. Tell them you like this cover, but you have a few ideas to change it up, and make it your own. You can also send your designer three or four covers you like to let them know this is the style you're thinking of.

Sometimes I know exactly what I want. When that happens I put together a short sketch explaining it. Other times, I let the designer know I have no idea what I want. When this is the case, I normally select four or five designers to create a concept for me. If none of the designs that come back are exactly what I'm looking for I'll try again. Sometimes I might like different portions of several covers, and I have one of the designers put it all together for me.

Most recently, I've been more concerned about controlling the images used on my book covers. Some designers on Fiverr have an upcharge to purchase clipart for you, but you never know. If they grab a piece of art without the proper license, it's your butt that's on the line for a lawsuit. Another issue I've run into is I don't remember which designer I used to make some of my earlier covers. This creates problems when I release audio books and paperbacks, because I don't know where to purchase clipart rights for the newer versions of those covers.

Because of this I've begun sourcing most of the clipart for my covers myself before giving the project to a designer. This way I know I'm legal, and hold the proper licenses for all of the art work used on my covers. I get most of my clipart from Can Stock Photo, http://www.canstockphoto.com/. Their prices are reasonable and range from $2.50 to $10.00 per use.

I don't claim to be a lawyer or anything, but keep in mind, you need to pay each time you use a piece of clipart. So if your book is available as an eBook, paperback, and audio book, you need to purchase the rights to the clipart three separate times.

After I've picked out the images to use, I put together specific instructions for the cover designer.

I would like a book cover for an Audible audio book. The cover size is 2500 x 2500 pixels. It needs to be a perfect square, and all of the text and images need to be fitted to it. You cannot stretch out the original book cover to fit the space. They will reject the cover.

I am enclosing the original clipart, and a copy of the original book cover. Please keep as close to the original design as possible.

Be sure to specify the exact cover size you want. Even when you order an eBook cover, every designer seems to deliver it in slightly different dimensions. When you order a Create Space cover, make sure you let the designer know it needs to be delivered as a .pdf file, and that it needs to conform to the Create Space sizing guidelines. I've had several designers deliver the paperback cover as a jpeg, and as a result it was unusable.

When you order a paperback cover for Create Space you need to specify the trim size (example: 6 x 9), the paper style (cream or white), the page style (black and white or color), and how many pages are in your book. Your designer requires all this information to properly size your cover. You will also need to supply any text or illustrations for the back cover blurb. If you want printing on the spine you need to specify the text. **FYI**: Your book needs to be at least 120 pages to have room for a printed message on the spine.

If you're not sure about your cover or your book concept, it can be a good idea to have several covers ready to go. That way if your book gets off to a slow start you can switch covers and see which one does a better job.

Write a compelling book description. Congratulations. You've done it. You've written an awesome title. You created a dazzling book cover. Now you've just got to close the deal.

How do you turn browsers into buyers?

A compelling book description can get readers drooling for more.

There's no right or wrong way to write a book description.

Some authors start off b asking a question. Others present a dilemma that either their reader or their main character may find themselves in. Still others summarize their story. Any of these approaches can work.

What you want to do is draw readers in. Get them hooked on your story, or in the case of nonfiction, on the solution you're presenting. Make it interesting. Create suspense. Make sure they want to read more.

How do you do that?

Ask questions.

Have you ever wondered what life would be like if you took the other road? The one your parents, teachers, and friends told you would put you on a collision course with the others? What if you veered just a little off course, for just a few minutes? Would it change your destiny forever?

Make your case as an authority figure.

Fifteen years as an eBay Power Seller and Top Rated Seller gives Nick a unique combination of experience and knowledge to guide new and experienced sellers through the maze we call eBay.

Introduce your main character.

Max Power stood at the crossroads of now and forever. If he followed her into the time portal everything behind him would disappear forever. If he took the leap his future would be uncertain. All Max knew for certain was the girl had saved his life back on Zeta 9. Now she was offering him a future as uncertain as the Zonderan Divide.

Compare your writing to a famous author.

Reviewers say my writing is a cross between Stephen King and Peter Straub with a touch of Kurt Vonnegut thrown in for comedy relief. Read Death Race 3000, and find out for yourself why the Zombie Jesus challenged the Werewolf Devil. Laugh your ass off. Puke your guts out. Run the full gamut of your emotions. You may never want to read another book again – Ever!

F A B Approach.

In sales terms you need to F – A – B prospective book buyers and offer them the Features, Advantages, and Benefits of reading your book.

For example:

Feature: This book offers a simple step-by-step plan to succeed in selling on eBay.

Advantage: What this means to you is you will have a detailed and tested plan to follow

Benefit: so you can easily make $100 a day or more selling on eBay.

The beauty of the F – A – B System is it makes everything easy for the reader to understand. In this example, you are offering "a simple step-by-step plan to succeed on eBay." Then you follow up and tell the reader "What this means to you" (you have to tell them, don't ever assume they get it) "is you will have a detailed and tested plan to follow." Sounds good so far, but you still haven't told them what's in it for them. You need to clearly tell them what following your system will do for them. In this case, it means they "can easily make $100 a day or more selling on eBay."

Let's look at another example:

Feature: The weight loss advice in this book allows you to eat all of the foods you like.

Advantage: What this means for you is that you won't start to feel deprived of your favorite foods, and get the urge to cheat on your diet.

Benefit: As a result you will be more likely to follow through with the plan, and drop those pounds you want to lose.

In the weight loss example, you are offering the reader weight loss advice, where they can eat all of the foods they like. Most people (at this point) are going to think that's great, but how can that be true. And you offer the advantage, because you won't "get the urge to cheat on your diet." Then you follow up with the benefit, and let them know what's in it for them – because "you're more likely to follow through with the plan," it will be easier for you to drop the pounds you want to lose.

You can add more information, and explain some of the details of your plan. A great way to do this is with a series of bullet points. Lists make it easy for readers to see what you're offering. They're easy to scan and readers can go right to the points that interest them.

Another method is to use bold headlines to break out your offer.

. Under each headline include two or three short sentences describing your offer.

. The key is to make it easy for readers to go right to the information that interests them.

When you write a nonfiction book description—it's all about the reader. If you can show readers you can help them get what they want, you will have them eating out of your hands.

Choose keywords that attract buyers. The easiest way to understand keywords is to think of them as mini billboards that drive searchers to your books.

Amazon has several areas where you can add keywords to optimize traffic to your book.

1. The book title and subtitle
2. The book description
3. The search keywords you enter when you upload your book

If you're totally new to keyword optimization, your first question is probably going to be, "What are keywords, and how do I find the right ones to describe my book?"

A lot of the "experts" recommend you use the Google Keywords tool, but that really isn't necessary. The best way to optimize your book for Amazon, is to use Amazon's search tools.

Nine times out of ten, I select most of my search terms using the Amazon search bar. It shows me the terms readers use to find similar books on Amazon.

Go to the Amazon search bar, click on the arrow at the left hand side, and select Kindle Store. Type in your general search term. In this case—"eBay."

What pops up is –

- eBay in Kindle Store
- eBay in all departments
- eBay in Apps for Android
- eBay selling
- eBay for dummies
- eBay .com
- eBay business
- eBay garage sale
- eBay home
- eBay books
- eBay store
- eBay 2014

These are the search terms potential readers are going to click on. *eBay for Dummies* and *eBay 2014* can't be used in your seven search terms, because they are titles of books in the category. It is against Amazon's TOS to use book titles or author names in your search keywords.

Some of the keywords I would use are: eBay selling, eBay business, eBay garage sale, eBay books, and eBay store.

Next type in "eBay" followed by each letter of the alphabet, and cull out search terms you think would be relevant to your book.

When I did this here are some of the other keywords I came up with –

- eBay Amazon
- eBay arbitrage
- eBay buying and selling
- eBay basics
- eBay consignment
- eBay clothing
- eBay drop shipping
- eBay guide
- eBay how to
- eBay income
- eBay power seller
- eBay shipping

This gives us seventeen solid keywords readers searching for Kindle books are actually using. You can further validate these keywords by looking at book titles and descriptions.

Type "eBay" into the Amazon search bar, and select the first book. Go down to the product details section. Most of the books will be ranked in two or three categories. Select the category labeled eBay, and this will take you into the eBay bestsellers.

Look through the titles and descriptions for the books listed, and you can easily determine which keywords other authors determined to be most relevant. Use this info to narrow down your search terms.

Ensure that your "look inside" sample closes the deal. It's the top of the ninth, bases are loaded, and the suspense is building. Can you convert lookers into a buyer?

You're batting 100 so far. You've written a great book. Your cover, title, and keywords convinced readers to click on your book. They've read over your description, but they're not sure. Should they buy it? Should they search for another book? Or should they take a "look inside" and see what your book is all about?

This is your last chance to hook your reader and get them to press the buy button. You need to make sure your "look inside" sample puts your best foot forward.

If you write fiction, it needs to be suspenseful. Don't waste any words laying out scenes or scenarios. Jump right into your story. Come out with both guns blazing. Keep the action building, and end your sample on a cliffhanger where readers just have to buy the book to discover what happens next.

If you write nonfiction, open your book with a "Why you need to read this book" section. Outline the problem your book is going to solve for readers, and present the steps you're going to take to relieve their pain. Follow this up with a short "About me" section where you introduce yourself, your qualifications, and why you're the best guy to solve their problem.

This is where longer books have a real advantage when it comes to helping you convert browsers into buyers.

Amazon samples the first ten percent of your book in the "look inside" feature. If you're book is short prospective readers will only be able to read one or two pages of your book. That's going to make it a tough sell. You really want readers to see your table of contents, and read at least, eight to ten pages of your book. The more they read, the more likely it is they will buy your book.

Combined with your title, cover, and description a good sample will help you sell more books.

On Amazon Promotions

Amazon offers several ways to promote your book. Some like KDP Free Promotions, Kindle Countdown Deals, and price are under your direct control. Others, such as promotional boxes, and direct mail newsletters, are more affected by how well your book sells.

I'm going to talk a little about each of these methods, and how you can best use them to sell more books on Amazon.

KDP Free Days are the first thing most authors think of when the talk turns to on Amazon promotions for your Kindle book. There's been a lot of talk recently that KDP Free Days aren't what they used to be, and there's some truth to that. But the fact is there are still a lot of authors who have been able to successfully launch or revive their books using KDP Free Days.

Amazon introduced Kindle Countdown Deals as a way for authors to promote their books without giving away the farm. The nice thing is they let you discount your book for up to seven days in every ninety day period. And, the best part is, even if you promote your book for 99¢, you receive the full 70 percent royalty, not 35 percent.

Kindle Unlimited is a great way to let readers sample your books, with virtually no risk. Amazon members, who are enrolled in Kindle unlimited, can read all the books they want for a low fee of only $9.99 per month. The problem for authors is Kindle Unlimited downloads make up fifty to seventy percent of sales in many categories. At .0058 cents per page read that can quickly eat away at your author earnings.

Price is a promotional tool you have available to you every day. Many authors keep their book sales steady by constantly cycling prices. When sales are good they leave their book prices at $2.99 or $3.99. When sales start to slow down they drop their book prices to 99¢ for from three to seven days to get sales moving again.

As I said, these are all promotions you affect and can set into motion at any time.

Once your book starts selling, Amazon's promotional algorithms kick in. The more books you sell the harder Amazon works to promote your book.

When your book is first released you have the opportunity to win one of the three coveted Hot New Releases spots at the top of Amazon's sales page. In some categories as few as one to two sales per day will win you the box. In more competitive categories it may take thirty or more sales per day. It also comes down to luck. If you release your book when there are fewer new titles being released it will be easier for your book to make the Hot New Releases section.

Books are only eligible to be on the Hot New Releases list for thirty days after publication. I've seen some authors game the system by changing the publication date of their book every month. This way they can stay on the Hot New Releases list for two or three months, rather than one. Should you do it? Probably not. If Amazon catches wind of it, they can delete your book or close your Kindle account.

As more of your books sell Amazon will promote them in the Customers who bought this item also bought section. This spot gives your book more exposure to readers who may have an interest in it. The more books you sell, the more people Amazon will promote your book to.

Amazon also sends out promotional emails several times per week. Sometimes they promote just one book, and other times they promote a group of similar books. When your book gets on one of these lists it can mean a lot of extra sales.

Again, you can only affect Amazon's promotions indirectly, because the Amazon marketing engine runs on sales. Some authors try to game the system by joining groups of authors that agree to purchase each-others books over a short period of time to try and raise their sales rank. Other authors buy fifty or one hundred copies of their own book all at once thinking this will raise their rank. The only problem is Amazon has caught on to this game. Large groups of books purchased all at once or in a short period of time are counted as a single purchase when determining seller rankings.

Lesson learned: Only real sales count, quit trying to game the system and concentrate on marketing your books to real readers.

KDP Free Days

KDP Free Days are the old stand by for launching your Kindle book, and for reinvigorating a book with sluggish sales.

There's a lot of talk among authors that free has lost its allure, and books are no longer enjoying the sales bump they used to enjoy after a great free run. Part of that is true, but it doesn't necessarily mean that running a free promo can't help your book.

It just means you need to better understand what results you can expect to receive from your free run.

If you're launching a new book, free is still one of the best ways to get the word out there, and to get people reading, and talking about your book.

If you've already run through two or three KPD Free Promos, free may no longer be the best option for you. One, because with so many new books being added to the Amazon catalog every day, it's getting harder, and harder, to get noticed; and two, with recent changes to how free books are counted towards sales numbers, a free promo (even a wildly successful one), isn't going to give your book the sales bump you were hoping for.

Let me give you an example. I recently ran a three day free promo for my book, *History Bytes*. It received over 25,000 downloads, and ranked number three in the Kindle Free Store. Over the next three weeks it sold 250 copies, and received another 40,000 page reads. Not bad, but…based on the number three rank when it came off Free, I expected better.

Most authors today agree you can't just select a free promo, and expect thousands of downloads to follow. You need to aggressively promote your KDP Free Days.

You need to blog about your free promo days. You need to jump on Facebook and Twitter to help spread the word. Some authors purchase ads on Bookbub, Pixel of Ink, and other popular sites.

I've seen list after list of sites you can promote your free books on. The problem is these sites come and go quickly, so lists go out of date almost as soon as they're posted. An easier way to promote your book is to purchase four or five Fiverr gigs, and let them do the promotional work for you. This will save you a lot of time, frustration, and wasted emails.

Here are some of the better Fiverr gigs I've used.

- http://www.fiverr.com/koky1205/submit-your-free-kindle-book-to-20-best-kindle-promotion
- http://www.fiverr.com/mlmauthor/promote-your-free-kindle-book
- http://www.fiverr.com/thedesertgirl/submit-your-free-kindle-book-to-12-promo-sites
- http://www.fiverr.com/bknights/submit-your-free-kindle-book-to-the-15-best-kindle-promotion-sites
- http://www.fiverr.com/timmybx/manually-submit-your-kdp-kindle-ebook-free-day-promo-to-15-kindle-book-sites

So what's an author to do?

Remember KDP is only one option you have available in your toolbox.

Steve Scott published a great book called *Is 99 Cents the New Free?* For several months after it was published just about every kindle author was knocking the idea around, and sampling their catalog at 99 cents.

Jordan Malik made a hell of a run using 99 cent promos in the eBay category three times in the last six months. Each time he brought his books up to number one, two, and three in the eBay category, and held the top position for nearly a week. When he ended the promo he returned his books to $6.99, and still ranked high in his category.

How did he do it? I finally stopped wondering, and did a little research. I found the answer on his Amazon author page. His most recent blog post told me everything I needed to know. It advised readers, "99 cent sale (hurry!) – every one of my Kindle eBooks…"

If you haven't started building an email list, this should convince you why you need to start. Smart marketers reach out to their emails lists every day to launch new books, boost titles with sagging sales, and to discover what readers want next.

If you want to learn more about email marketing, read *Email Marketing Blueprint, The Ultimate Guide to Building an Email List Asset* by Steve Scott.

Indie Author's Toolbox

Using Kindle Countdown Deals

There seems to be a lot of confusion about how to best use the Kindle Countdown Deal.

Some authors don't understand how to use it; some worry about it not being available in all areas; others look at it as a watered down work around for KDP Free Days.

First we need to take a look at exactly what the Countdown Deal is. In Amazon's own words it's a "new KDP Select benefit that lets authors provide readers with limited time discount promotions on their books available on Amazon.com and Amazon.UK. It's a great opportunity to earn more royalties and increase discoverability of your book. Customers will see the regular price and the promotional price on the book's detail page, as well as a countdown clock showing how much time is left at the promotional price. You'll also continue to earn your selected royalty rate on each sale during the promotion."

A quick read through of Amazon's description will answer many of the questions authors have about using Kindle Countdown Deals.

First off, it's a limited time promotion. You can set the time period you want it to run – anywhere from one hour to seven days. You can also set the discount levels. If your book is $3.99 you can split the promotion over three levels. Your book would start out at 99 cents and increase in price by one dollar increments evenly split across the time period for the promo. The timer resets for every price level, showing how long buyers have to purchase your book at the discounted price.

Some of the complaints I've heard are it's too confusing; or there should be just one price point – 99 cents for the entire promo; or the counter is too cheesy, or pushy. I think this ignores the whole point of the Countdown Deal. It's the urgency of the timer ticking away that makes readers rush in to buy now, before the price moves to the next level. If you take away the timer, sales are going to nosedive. If you only want one discounted price for the entire Countdown Deal, you have complete control over that. When you are offered a choice of sale increments you would choose one.

Another area authors are concerned about is the deal is not available to everyone; just to readers in limited areas. Martin Crosbie talked about this in an *Indies Unlimited* blog post saying he had problems changing prices worldwide so no one would feel left out. The point is, Amazon has chosen to make the Countdown Deal available exclusively to book buyers in the United States and United Kingdom. It's an Amazon thing. Authors shouldn't feel obligated to figure out how to make the deal available to readers in areas where Amazon didn't intend to extend it. If you run an ad to promote your Countdown Deal, and are concerned international readers will want the discounted price, you can state something to the effect, "Amazon only makes the deal available in the United States, and United Kingdom." I've noticed Steve Scott does this in his blog posts when he mentions his Countdown Deals. He tells readers if they're from an area that doesn't have them to email him, and he'll see what he can do.

A number of authors have said they don't intend to use it because they've heard from others that it didn't work for them. That's putting the cart before the horse. Just because it didn't work for Stephen King, or some other author, doesn't mean it won't work for you. Listen to what other authors have to say, but don't let them make decisions for you. Try every available tool out for yourself. If it doesn't work, discard it. If it does work, add it to your toolbox.

KDP Free days don't work for every author either. It all comes down to the book you are promoting; the days you are promoting it on; whether other authors in your genre are running deals at the same time; and a good dose of luck.

Let me give you an example. I ran my first Countdown Deal several years ago. I tried it with ten of my books. One of them moved seventy-five books in the seven day period, and another sold sixty-five copies. That was two to three times the number of books I sold the week before without running the Countdown Deal. Not too shabby. Five of my other books sold from five to fifteen copies during their seven day run, and three of my books didn't sell a single copy during their Countdown Deal.

Overall, I was happy with the results. The two books with the best sales sustained their initial bump in sales for almost a month, and remained among the top five sellers in their category.

The best indicator the Countdown Deal worked came from my Kindle sales and commission reports. Total Kindle sales were up 250 copies for the month and my royalties rocketed up nearly $300 from the previous month. Create Space royalties shot up over $700 for the month, but I have no way of tying that to the Countdown Deal.

Would I run the Countdown Deal again? It's a no brainer. Yes I would, and I am doing it right now. The two best books from my last promotion, *eBay 2014* and *eBay Unleashed*, are having a good run again. One surprise seller is *Abraham Lincoln: The Baltimore Plot*. Both of my KDP Free Day promos for it failed to give away over a few hundred copies, and sales never took off. Before this promo I probably never sold over five copies in seven months of trying to promote it. In the first three days of the Countdown Deal it's sold twenty-one copies. This may be the breakout it needs to start selling.

Sales for the two eBay books would have been much higher this time around, but one of the heavy hitters in the eBay category, Steve Weber, ran the Countdown Deal on his three bestselling books for the same period I chose to run mine. Luck wasn't on my side this time, but its ok - I still had a great promo. Sales of *eBay*

2014 are still going strong two days after the Countdown Deal for it ended.

A lesson we can learn from Weber's Kindle Countdown Deal is the promo works amazingly well for bestselling books. His book *Barcode Booty* jumped from a 12,000 to 15,000 ranking in the Kindle Paid Store to around 1800. Three days later it's still hanging in there at around a 7800 ranking. For one day three of his books ranked one, two, and three in the eBay category. All of them were propelled there using the Countdown Deal.

Another author discussed the Kindle Countdown Deal in one of his blog posts. He said a few of his books sold several hundred copies during the promo, and kept going strong afterwards. Some of his books didn't do as well. He shared the same info about using Kindle Free Days. Sometimes they work, and sometimes they don't.

If you don't try it for yourself, you'll never know what works best for your books.

The final complaint I saw concerned royalties paid to authors during the Countdown Deal. Under the rules of the program you're supposed to be paid at the current royalty level for your book, either 35 or 70 percent. Some authors mentioned their royalties were paid at the lower level, and I did see some of this in my sales reports too. This may be a temporary reporting glitch, or it may be one of the kinks Amazon still has to work out.

Whatever else you can say Kindle Countdown Deals are a great promotional tool for authors. Unlike KDP Free Days, Kindle Countdown Deals can help you get extra sales, and make money too.

Authors need to keep close tabs every time they run a promo, and decide for each book which promo is going to do a better job – Free or discounted pricing.

I recently caught up with author Rob Parnell and got his take on Countdown Deals.

"From my perspective, Countdown Deals are much better than free days. I'm often stunned by how little difference it makes to give away thousands of books – especially because all the hype says it does so much good. Countdown Deals generate a lot of sales for me. Plus they keep you in the chart after the deal has expired."

Martin Crosbie told me he's "seeing results utilizing Kindle Countdown Deals through KDP Select. I run a three day promo with my book at 99¢ and I supplement the promo with an ad on Ereader News Today, Kindle Books and Tips or Bookbub."

Kindle Unlimited

Kindle Unlimited is Amazon's answer to free reading sites like Oyster and Scribd. For $9.99 subscribers can read an unlimited number of books, as long as the books they choose are enrolled in the program. It's a win-win for readers, and authors. For readers, they can sample new authors without any risks (other than their time). For authors, Kindle Unlimited is an inexpensive way to build your fanbase without having to shell out a bunch of cash.

If you haven't sampled Kindle Unlimited, it's easy to get started—just hop on over to Kindle Unlimited, and sign up for your subscription. It's that easy. Once you're signed up, you can download up to ten books at a time. After that, you're prompted to return a book for every book you want to borrow.

According to Amazon there are over one million books currently enrolled in Kindle Unlimited. Many are from large publishers, but the majority of selections are from self-publishers like you and me.

For the longest time, I enrolled over ninety percent of my books in Kindle Unlimited. With the recent changes where they switched from paying per book to per page read (August 2015), I moved most of them back out of Kindle Unlimited. The reason is, I write mostly short books—under 100 pages, and it doesn't make sense to let Amazon give them away, and avoid paying me a fair royalty. Sorry, it's a personal preference. I work hard putting my books together, and I expect to get paid well for the work I do.

Kindle Unlimited is a hot mess right now. If you write longer books (over 200 pages) you will be okay. If you write short books

(25 to 100 pages) the newest change to Kindle Unlimited is going to be a drain on your pocket book.

With its latest incarnation (August 2015) the payout for Kindle Unlimited reads went from roughly $1.41 per borrow, to .0058 cents per page. What that means for authors is if your book is fifty pages long, you're royalty payout is 29 cents. If your book is 100 pages long, you're going to receive 58 cents in royalties.

Youch! That stings.

If you write short books, it's time for a change in strategy. You can write longer books, or do what I did—pull your shorter works out of KDP, and publish them on other sites.

I understand why Amazon made this move. A lot of authors were gaming the system. Under the old rules, if readers flipped through ten percent of the pages in a book—authors got paid. Because of that, a lot of authors created short books of ten to twenty pages. Readers only had to flip through one or two pages, and the author got paid.

The thing is, Amazon is smarter than that. They know when people are gaming the system, and they close the gaps as quick as people open them. They shut down authors who found a workaround using HTML code to add pictures and videos to their book descriptions, and again with authors who cheated on reviews, and purchased false reviews to make their books look better.

Off Amazon Promotions

After you've got all of your ducks in a row on Amazon, it's time to decide what comes next.

For many authors, the answer is nothing. They continue to tweak their Amazon book description page, cycle prices up and down to smooth out the rough periods, and switch things up by using a combination of KDP Free days and Kindle Countdown Deals.

Other authors swear they couldn't do it without the help of Facebook, Twitter, goodreads, Pinterest, and more.

Who's right?

The real answer is, there is no right, or wrong answer. Some of it is a matter of preference. Some of it depends on the type of books you write. A lot of it comes down to dumb luck.

I'm going to say up front, I'm one of those guys who let's Amazon do most of the work for me. I spend a lot of time tweaking my book descriptions, switching up the extra content sections, and tightening up my author bio. Sometimes I change out the covers on my books to see if that will drive more sales. I rewrite and revise many of my books regularly, especially the first few chapters that appear in my "look inside" preview.

I don't use Google to find new books. Nine times out of ten I wouldn't go out of my way to search out a book someone touted on Facebook, or in a blog post. So why should I waste all of that time on social media?

I don't really have a good answer. Except – I read about guys like Martin Crosbie who says how much Facebook helped him, especially some of the author groups who helped skyrocket his book all the way to number one during its first free run. I see Steve Scott using Facebook and SlideShare more often. And, I get to thinking like the Grinch – Maybe there's more to this social media thing than meets the eye.

With that thought in mind, I'm going to give you my take on social media.

Keep in mind what I say here is just one guy's opinion. Don't invest a hundred hours or a hundred dollars into something until you're sure it's something that's going to work for you, and that it's something you're comfortable using.

Social Media

The talk among authors is you can't strike it big without a major social media presence.

I'm not sure whether that's true or not. I look at social media as another trick you hold in your toolbox. It can help build your author brand. It may even help you sell more books. But before any of that can happen, you need to develop a plan.

Without a plan social media can become a major time suck that keeps authors from doing what's most important – writing another book.

Success in social media isn't about posting to Facebook every half hour, or sending out dozens of tweets every day. It's about building a connection with readers that makes them want to keep coming back for more, and maybe, just maybe – want to check out a few of your books.

So how do you do that? Stress quality over quantity. Research shows the most shared posts are images, or short videos. What this tells you is if you want to get more shares you need to post short image oriented items.

Make a crazy face while you're pointing at a headline in a newspaper or magazine. If you're on a round-the-world, or round-the-city tour, post a bunch of selfies of yourself standing by local monuments or statues. Photoshop yourself standing next to President Obama, Captain Kirk, or one of your literary heroes. Insert one of those bubble captions with a quote from one of your books, or some crazy thought that just popped into your head.

Make it fun! Make it worth checking back every day to see what's next. Develop a reputation for presenting strange news, crazy facts, or just telling it like it is.

Over the last ten years every time I go to tell my kids something stupid, I preface it with the words "interesting dinosaur factoid #____." Giving my stupidity a title helps build the conversation and makes it something they look forward to hearing more of.

If I was to translate that to Facebook, I could have a little dinosaur dude drawn up with the words "interesting dinosaur factoid" and insert the number in my post. If I was to do it consistently I'd likely build up a following of fans who keep returning to find out what crazy thing I was going to say next.

What about you? You don't have to do anything crazy, or stupid.

If you write about history, you could post a simple factoid about "today in history" or "this week in history." Grab a piece of clipart or a public domain image, and slap up some juicy tidbits of history that your readers might be unaware of.

If you're a fiction writer, write a Facebook novel. Post short 100 or 200 word chapters every few days. If you write historical thrillers set in medieval days post pictures of European castles, knights on horseback, and damsels in distress. Grab YouTube clips from Renaissance Festivals and post them to your timeline.

There are all sorts of interesting things out there your fans would be interested in learning about.

If you really want to be successful with social media you need to give more than you get. The majority of your posts should entertain and educate your fans. After you've earned the right, you can mention your free book or Kindle Countdown Deal, but you need to follow it up by giving your followers more information they can use.

Explaining how to use the individual social media sites is beyond the range of this book.

The big players as I write this are Facebook, Twitter, LinkedIn, Pinterest, and Instagram. Some authors like to establish a presence on all of them. My suggestion is to select one or two social media sites that interest you. Set aside a half an hour, or an hour a week, to slowly build your brand. One or two posts per week should do when you're getting started.

Reviving a dead book

It's natural for book sales to slow down over time. It's just the way it works.

Summer is a slow time for book sales – period. If your book sales slowdown between May and August you should probably just shrug your shoulders and let it go. Maybe run a Countdown Deal, or feature your book at 99¢ for a few days every month to keep your sales going. If things don't pick up by September then you may want to attempt more drastic methods to resuscitate your book.

After a while Amazon starts shaking up categories, and begins to feature newer books. They don't want their inventory to get stale, and they understand readers prefer newer books. If you're willing to do a little work, you can make this change work for you too. The trick is to bring out a new edition of your book. Revise your book. Add new information. Write a new introduction that summarizes updates in the field since your book was first published.

If you write fiction, open your bag of tricks and add new content to your book. How about appending an alternate ending; providing a character outline; or including additional chapters that bring more depth to one of your minor characters.

Once you've made these changes update your book cover and description to reflect that you have new and revised content available. In the KDP dashboard list this version of your book as the second edition, and change the publication date so it shows the date of your revision. In effect, you're releasing a new book, without all the extra work.

The following case study talks about how I revised and rebranded several of my eBay guides last fall.

Case Study

What do you do when the subject you write about is constantly changing?

Do you sidestep the issues of pricing, fees, and changing policies? Do you concentrate on the basics, because you're afraid to give specific advice that will date your book? Do you dive head first into the fray, and give specifics knowing the information you give will be outdated in six months or a year?

That was the dilemma I found myself in last November. Most of my eBay guides were becoming dated. They still sold well, and ranked in the top ten or twenty books in their category. But, I noticed a lot of new books being published in my niche. They did the same thing. They danced around the issue of fees and policy updates.

I gave it a lot of thought. Many of my reviews said readers wanted to know more about what it costs to sell on eBay. They wanted to know about how eBay's new and changing policies affected their business, and what the changes meant for them going forward.

Over the period of a month, I revised four of my books. I rewrote at least twenty percent of each book, added a new introduction, and had new covers designed for each of them. One of the books I totally rebranded. I gave it a new title, changed the contents around, and rewrote major portions of it.

That one went on to become my bestselling books, *eBay 2014*.

Another one of my books really worried me.

eBay Unleashed had always sold well. I rebranded it with a new cover, and made minor changes inside to reflect eBay's new policies, but no major changes. The first two months the revised version was out sales dropped by over twenty-five percent. I don't know how many times I was tempted to roll all of the revisions back, but I didn't. From hindsight, I can look back and be glad I waited it out. Sales bounced back, and it's a consistent money-maker, bringing in $800 to $1,000 per month in royalties.

I don't think any of them would be selling this well if I hadn't taken a chance and revised them.

What else can you do to resuscitate a dead book? Many times a few minor changes can help your book sell more copies. The trick to increasing sales is to monitor your sales, and determine when sales first started dropping off. Sometimes it can mean a competing book entered your niche, and readers are buying it rather than your book. If this is the case, you need to examine that book, and determine why it's selling better.

Does it have a better title? Is the description more enticing? Maybe the content is more up-to-date than yours?

Be honest with yourself. If the problem is a new book in your category, the best thing to do might be to do nothing. Over the last three years I've watched dozens of new books jump ahead of mine in the eBay category. Most of them run their course in a month or less, and slip back down the charts. If the problem is more persistent, take a look at the description for both books. Sometimes if you tweak your description just a little, you can make your book seem more attractive to readers.

Other times, your price may be the problem. When I first started selling my books on Kindle I was able to price them at $4.87. As the eBay category became more crowded I was forced to drop my prices to $2.99 to remain competitive. At one point a number of authors in my category decided to slug it out, and priced their books at 99¢, hoping to reach the number one spot on the charts. I decided to stay out of that battle, and let them give their books away for nothing. I didn't want to be a bestseller that bad.

Sometimes it may be just the opposite problem. If all the other books in your category are priced between $5.99 and $9.99, and yours is selling for $2.99, readers are going to ask themselves what's wrong with your book. Try raising the price a few dollars. That might be all it takes to get your sales going again.

Change your title, or cover. Here's another secret big publishers use.

Have several versions of your cover made up when you publish your book. Run the first cover for two weeks. If sales aren't what you expect, switch it out. See if a different cover sells more books. Sometimes a slightly different background color can increase sales. Other times, an entirely different cover can boost lagging book sales.

The same thing goes for your title. A bad title can tank your sales. I named one of my books *My eBay Sales Suck: How to really make money selling on eBay*. It did ok. Most months it sold sixty to one hundred copies, but I always thought it could do better. After a giving it a lot of thought, I changed the title *to eBay 2014: Why you're not selling anything on eBay and what you can do about it*. Since that change it sells close to two hundred copies every month.

When all else fails. Some books won't sell on Amazon, no matter what you do. That doesn't mean they're bad books. It just means you need to market them differently.

At the end of last year I created a new series of career search books titled *Find a Job Fast*. I did one for Iowa, one for Illinois, and one for California. The Iowa and Illinois version haven't sold a single copy. The California version sold three copies.

Talk about a bunch of dogs. I spent months putting this series together, and nothing. Zip!

After a lot of thought, I think I've finally developed several marketing plans where these books can make some good money.

Listen up, and let me know what you think about these ideas. Hit me up at hi@nickvulich.com.

1. Present a job search seminar at local libraries, YMCA's, and community colleges. Sell the guides to participants after the class.
2. Develop a series of branded job hunt guides for local colleges. Get employers to sponsor advertising in the books, and give them away through college recruiting offices.
3. Brand the book for different cities. Sell ads to local employers, and give the books away for free at libraries, schools, convenience stores, and such.

Key takeaway: If your book isn't selling, it's up to you to revive it. Strap on your thinking cap, and step up your marketing.

Publishing beyond Amazon

Kindle, Print, or Audio, Which format is more important to your success?

It seems to me a lot of Kindle authors are doing it all wrong. They have this tenacious focus on eBooks believing that print is dead.

The truth is anything but that. Yes, a lot of people have moved on to the new technology and wouldn't dream of serving all their new books up on anything but an e-reader. The thing is there are still a lot of people out there who like to read their books old style. They enjoy the feel of a book in their hands. They want to highlight their favorite passages; they want to make notes in the margins; and they just love to fold the corners to mark their favorite pages. Some people like it both ways. They like the feel of a good book in their hands for those lazy days around the house, but they load up their Kindles for when they're on the go. Amazon recognized this when they created their Kindle Match-Book program. It lets readers pick up free, or discounted eBooks, when they purchase the print version.

What authors need to understand is readers appreciate a choice. How'd that old candy bar jingle put it, "Sometimes you feel like a nut, sometimes you don't." Camille Picott in her book, *Indie Publishing Essentials,* touches on this same subject. She tries to make all her books available in print, eBook, and audio format, because she never knows how readers are going to want her book served up. She writes that many months her audio books outsell the Kindle and print editions.

How about you? If you're books are only available on Kindle, how many dollars are you missing out on in lost royalties? How many book sales are you losing out on because you're not offering readers a choice?

The majority of my books are available as eBooks, paperbacks, and audio books.

While my Kindle books outsell print copies by a margin of two or three to one, my paperback royalties from Create Space consistently exceed my kindle royalties.

Kindle authors, here is my question for you. How many dollars are you leaving on the table, if you aren't making your books available in print?

Create Space

CreateSpace **is an Amazon company** that gives authors a low cost option for producing paperback versions of their books.

Getting started with Create Space is easy. The first step is to determine the trim size you want to make your book available in. The suggested trim size for trade paperbacks on Create Space is 6 inches x 9 inches. This will ensure your books can be sold through the most outlets possible. Create Space lets you choose from 15 different trim sizes. Here is the link if you want to check them out https://www.createspace.com/Products/Book/.

After you've chosen a trim size for your book you need to format it. The easiest way to format your Create Space book is to use MS Word.

First off you need to choose a font. I've had good luck using Times New Roman and Calibri, but many professionals recommend Garamond or Book Antiqua. Format a chapter of your book using each font and decide which one you like best.

After this you're going to need to set your page margins. Before you get started, make a duplicate copy of your manuscript and work from it. This way if something goes wrong you can easily recover from it. Go to Page Layout – Size – More paper sizes, and manually select the page size you want. I normally set my margins to 0.50 all around. Keep in mind if you have a larger book you may want to adjust this to fit more text on each page. Create Space charges you based on how many pages are in your book so the fewer pages you use the cheaper the cost to print your book.

Now you need to number your pages. Go to Insert – Page Number, and select the style of page numbers you want to use. I like to use Bottom of Page – Accent Bar 1 because I can include the book title at the bottom of every page.

Choose your line spacing and paragraph indents. Most nonfiction books use block spacing with a line between paragraphs. Works of fiction generally use paragraph indents with no space between paragraphs. I use paragraph indents and a line between paragraphs when I format my books. I think it gives them a better look. There are no hard and fast rules. If you have a large book you may want to use paragraph indents with no space between paragraphs to save on printing costs.

If you're using images in your book ensure they are all high resolution images (300 DPI). Low resolution images can sometimes appear blurry or grainy, and Create Space will single them out later in the proofing process.

This will give you a good basic manuscript you can upload to Create Space that will pass their automated system check. If you want your book to have a more professional look similar to a traditionally published book I would suggest hiring a professional formatter. They will ensure all of your chapters begin on the right hand page, and all of your front and back matter are professionally formatted. If you're a do-it-yourselfer check out *Self-Publishing: How to Publish like a Pro for a Fraction of the Cost* by Donna Joy Usher.

Getting Started with Create Space

Before you can start listing books on Create Space you need to register. Go to https://www.createspace.com/ and select Sign up.

Log into your account, click on add new book in your member dashboard. In the Start your new project box type in the name of your project, select paperback, and where it says choose a setup process select guided (especially for your first book). Press get started to move to the next screen.

Fill out the basic information for your book – title, author, contributors, etc. if you're unsure how to answer any questions, click on what's this and it will give you directions. At the bottom of the page, click save and continue.

Next you're asked to choose an ISBN. You have four choices. Most authors choose to have Create Space assign a free ISBN for their book. You can purchase a custom ISBN from Create Space for ten dollars. If you have your own publishing company or imprint this is an inexpensive way to add a more professional look to your book. You can purchase a custom universal ISBN from Create Space for $99. This gives you more options than the generic ISBN. The difference is you can use the custom universal ISBN with other publishers, whereas if you purchase the regular custom ISBN it can only be used through Create Space. The final option is to provide your own ISBN. You can buy them through Bowker, or from online discounters.

Depending on the type of ISBN you purchase it can limit some of your distribution options. Any of them can be used with expanded distribution to help you sell more books. If you want to sell your books through libraries and educational institutions you need to use a Create Space assigned ISBN.

Select the option you want and follow the prompts for it. Click on assign ISBN to move to the next section. The next page you see shows you your ten digit and thirteen digit ISBN. A message pops up to tell you your ISBN is locked, and cannot be changed. If you want to change the title or author you need to assign your book a new ISBN.

Click on continue.

This section lets you select the trim size and interior of your book. The default trim size is 6 inches x 9 inches. If your book is a different size, select choose a different size, and pick the size you want to use. After this you need to choose an interior type – black and white or colored pages. Choose your page style – cream or white. Cream pages more closely resemble the look of a traditional book.

The next section lets you upload your book file. Choose upload your book file, and you will be prompted to choose a file. Manuscripts are accepted in these file formats -- .pdf, .doc, .docx, and .rtf. You're also offered the option of talking with someone from Create Space about professional design services. Costs start at $199 depending upon the amount of formatting involved.

While you're waiting for the interior file to upload and go through the automated print check you have the option to start working on your book cover while you wait, otherwise it takes a few minutes to process. When the automated print check is finished it will let you know if it found any errors. Click on launch interior reviewer to proof the contents of your book. You can page through your book and see what the final printing will look like. If everything appears ok, click on continue.

This section lets you work on your cover. First off, you need to select a finish for your cover – matte or glossy. Matte is a dull finish. Glossy is bright and shiny. For my money the matte finish makes a better looking book. After you've selected your cover type you need to select how you wish to submit your cover design. You have three options for this.

1. You can use the Create Space cover creator.
2. You can hire a professional cover designer from Create Space (starting at $399).
3. You can upload a PDF ready cover.

I'm not going to go into details on the Create Space cover designer. You can give it a shot, and see what you can turn out. Some of the styles are nice. It all comes down to whether you want to put a generic cover on your book, or give it a more professional appearance.

I would suggest hiring your own professional designer. There are several designers on Fiverr who do a good job, and will format your Create Space cover for ten to twenty dollars. Two of them I've had good luck working with are –

- http://www.fiverr.com/rroxx/create-awesome-professional-ebook-cover-design
- http://www.fiverr.com/vikncharlie/design-you-an-awesome-book-cover

If you're uploading your own book cover select browse to choose your file, and click on save. The next page shows that your cover has been successfully uploaded. It also gives you the option to make changes. If you're happy with what you have click on continue.

Next submit your book for review. Before you submit your files you're given the option to edit files. If everything looks good select submit files for review. A pop up box appears telling you your files are being checked. Click on continue to select your distribution options.

Your books are automatically listed for sale on Amazon.com, Amazon Europe, and the Create Space eStore. Royalties are larger when you sell through the Create Space eStore, so wherever possible link to it when you're selling copies of your own book.

The next section shows you the expanded distribution options. You can choose one, or all of these, depending upon how you want to make your book available.

Selecting Bookstores and online retailers makes your book available through online retailers. It takes about four to eight weeks for them to start selling on other sites, but when they finally show up your books will be available on Barnes & Noble, Books A Million, eBay, and others. You make less in royalties on each sale when they are sold through expanded distribution but you have the opportunity to reach more readers. In my case, I make between $250 and $300 per month from expanded distribution sales.

The Libraries and Academic institutions option lets you sell your books to schools and libraries. Create Space Direct makes your books available through independent bookstores and retailers. You're book isn't likely to appear on store shelves, but if customers request it a bookstore can order a copy for them.

After you've selected your distribution channels, click on save and continue.

Create Space shows a minimum price (you must charge at least this much for each book). Before you set your price play with the pricing tool and see what you will earn at different price points. If you selected expanded distribution, make sure you won't be losing money if you price your book too low. From what I understand Create Space will deduct any losses from your royalties.

If you write fiction a good price is probably somewhere between $7.95 and $12.95 depending upon what other books in your genre are selling for. If you're selling nonfiction you should be able to ask a higher price. I charge $15.99 for most of my eBay guidebooks. One of them sells a consistent one hundred copies per month. Several others sell twenty-five to fifty copies per month. I've seen other authors stretch their price to $19.99, or $25.99. The nice thing is you can change your prices at any time. Be warned: if your book is enrolled in expanded distribution it can sometimes take two to three months for the price to go back up.

When you're done pricing your book, click on save and continue.

The final step is to post your book description, categories, author bio and such. You're allowed to use a maximum of 4,000 characters in your description. You can use basic HTML to enhance your description – bold, italic, list, etc. To add a space between paragraphs you need to add the <br> code to add one line. To add two lines between paragraphs use

.

You're only allowed to choose one category so pick the one that best defines your book. Under additional information you can add your author bio. I copy and paste it from my Amazon Author page. Be sure to use HTML code to dress it up. Add the <br> code to add spacing between lines and paragraphs. Under search keywords you're able to enter five search terms. I believe the maximum character length is twenty-five, so keep that in mind when you are entering them. When you are finished with this section, click on save and continue.

At this point you're done entering your book information. You need to wait twelve to twenty-four hours for Amazon to check your files. When Create Space completes their automated file check they will email you with the results. If everything is ok you will be asked to proof your book. You can use the online proofer, download a PDF proof, or order a physical proof of your book.

Once you approve your proof your book will go live on Amazon. Most times Amazon will automatically associate your print book with your eBook. If they don't email customer service and they will get that taken care of for you.

After you've finished creating your Create Space book you have the option to have your book formatted and sold on Kindle. I've never used this option so I can't tell you exactly how it works.

Overall I've had a great experience using Create Space. My royalties per book are two to three times what I make selling a Kindle book and the best news is they pay royalties thirty days after they're earned.

FYI: Most times Amazon will discount your books by a few bucks to keep sales rolling in. The nice thing is, even when they discount the retail price of your book, they pay you royalties based on the full retail price.

It works the same way if another retailer drops their price, and Amazon lowers their price to match them. I had this happen with one of my books. Normal price was $12.99. Barnes & Noble dropped their price to $7.99 and Amazon matched it. I still received $5.62 in royalties per copy. The only exception was on copies sold through expanded distribution. My royalties for those sales were based on a $7.99 retail.

If you don't have a paperback version of your book I would encourage you to get one made.

Audible (ACX)

ACX is an Amazon company that sells books in the audio book format. They make audio books available on Audible, Amazon, and iTunes.

The least you need to know is audio books are still an emerging market. Compared to Amazon's twenty-five million plus titles, Audible has just 150,000 audio books available. Over the next five years that number is expected to grow to over one million audio books. That puts audio books in the same position Kindle was in three or four years ago. They're a growth market, and there's plenty of opportunity for good books, producers, and narrators.

Getting started on ACX is easy for authors.

Visit ACX.com. Midway down the page you will see an address bar that asks you to enter your ISBN, book title, or author name. After you do this ACX will display your book, or a list of your books. To get started click on the This is my book tab, and you will be taken to the next step in the process.

The next choice you're given is to select how you want to make your book available. The choices are:

1. I'm looking for someone to narrate and produce my audio book.
2. I have this book in audio and I want to sell it.
3. I will narrate my own book and upload it later.

The first option is what most authors should select. It will help you to find a qualified narrator to read and produce your book. When you select this option ACX shows you their book posting agreement. To proceed to the next step you need to read it over and click Agree & Continue.

On the next page you're going to need to fill in some general information about your book and who it is directed at. The book description is prepopulated for you with the information from your Amazon book page. Where it asks for copyright information normally you are the copyright owner for the book and for the audio book. Fill this information in along with the year of copyright.

Next you're asked if your book is fiction or nonfiction. Then you're asked to select the one category that best describes your book.

Below that you need to answer some general questions about the ideal narrator's voice you're looking for. Try to be as specific as possible when you're filling this section out. It will save you from listening to a lot of auditions that totally miss the mark on what you want.

Use the additional comments section to list more information about your book, or about what you are looking for in a narrator. When I listed my books I talked about their ranking on Amazon, how many books I was selling monthly and weekly, and how I was promoting them. Producers told me this information was a big help to them in choosing my books because it helped them decide if the project would pay off for them or not.

I considered a few of my books marginal, meaning they were only selling a few copies a month in Kindle or paperback. I let producers know that, and explained to them the books were short, easy to produce, and while they might not make a lot of money on the project it could be fun. I think producers appreciated my honesty. All eighteen of my projects were snapped up within a few days of listing them.

The last step on this page is to upload your audition script. You can upload a file, or link to a URL where you have the audition script located. ACX doesn't give you a character length to use as a guideline, but 4,000 characters is probably good. I generally upload three to five pages of text. When I listen to the audition for this it gives me a good idea of what the final book will sound like.

After you've uploaded your sample click ok at the bottom of the page and you will be directed to the final page of information ACX needs to collect.

At the top of this page you're asked to type in how many words are in your book. When you do this they estimate how many hours your final production will be.

Where it asks for territory rights put in the regions you hold the copyright for. The default response is world. If you only hold rights for one country or territory list that location instead.

The next section lets you choose how you want to pay for your production. There are two choices:

1. Royalty share. The narrator / producer covers the entire cost of production, and does all of the work associated with it. When the audio book goes up for sale you split royalties 50 / 50 with them. ACX handles all of the details and pays each of you separately. Your only responsibility is to upload a book cover (2500 x 2500 pixels).

2. Pay for production. You pay a narrator /producer to make the audio book for you, and in return you receive all royalties earned from sales of your audio book. If you choose this option you can enter the amount you are willing to pay per hour of finished audio. The going rate is $200 to $400 per finished hour, although I have seen some producers offering to work for as little as $50 per hour, and others listing their rates at $500 or more per finished hour.

After you select your payment method you are prompted to select the type of distribution you want. If you selected royalty share your only option is exclusive distribution through Audible,

Amazon, and iTunes. Your royalty is 40%, and it is split 50 / 50 between you and the producer.

If you paid for the production of your audio book you can choose non-exclusive distribution. This lets you sell through Audible, Amazon, iTunes, and other methods of your choice. Your royalty this way is 25% and you keep all of it.

After you've made these selections, click Save & Continue to move to the final page. This page summarizes your information and gives you the option to post your book's information to ACX.

If you already have the book on audio and want to distribute it through ACX, chose the second option – I have this book in audio and want to sell it. Follow the prompts to list your book through ACX. You need to choose the territory you have rights for, select exclusive distribution through ACX (40% royalty), or non-exclusive (25% royalty). After you do this, you move to the next page and agree to ACX's terms of service. The final page allows you to give information about your book, and post it for sale.

The last option is to record your own audio and upload your book yourself. If you choose to do this ACX offers a number of tips on how to do the best job possible. You may also want to check out How to Create an Audiobook for Audible by Rob Archangel and Buck Flogging. They explain the process in more detail and talk about the equipment you need to make a good recording.

My experience with ACX has been amazing. Their interface is easy to use. You are prompted to include the proper information every step of the way so it's unlikely you will mess anything up. Within hours of posting my books, I received dozens of auditions, many of them from producers with years of experience doing voiceover work and narrating eBooks. My first four books were ready and up for sale in less than three weeks. The first week my audio books were up for sale we sold fifty-eight copies.

The key to getting good results is to carefully listen to each of your auditions. Ask yourself if the narrator's voice and tone matches your book. Most often I know within the first ten seconds of listening to the audition if the narrator is a good fit for my book. Trust your gut. If it sounds good to you, it will probably sound good to other listeners.

If you're not sure about a narrator, pass on the audition. There are plenty of producers and narrators looking for good projects and they will find your book if you give them time.

Final thought. I listed eighteen audio books for production in the same week. As a result I went with the royalty share option on all of them. It saved me money up front, and it allowed me to get all the projects going at the same time. If I had it to do again, I would cherry pick my books, and pay for the production of my bestsellers up front. Over the long haul I would probably make thousands of dollars more in royalties.

Babelcube

M**ost authors receive** a number of international sales. About fifteen percent of my book sales come from the United Kingdom. Other countries account for another one to two percent of my sales.

Babelcube gives you an opportunity to increase sales in other countries by offering translations of your books. They currently offer translation services into Spanish, French, German, Italian, Portuguese, Japanese, and Chinese.

If you want to check out Babelcube follow this link http://www.babelcube.com/.

Babelcube connects writers with translators. It's easy to use. Just post your profile, upload information about your books, and wait for independent translators to contact you. For authors, there's no cost up front. Babelcube handles all of the details and splits the profits between you, the translator, and of course, they keep a small cut for the house.

Commissions are based on how much revenue your books take in. Babelcube takes 15% for brokering the deal. Your split ranges from 30% to 75% depending upon how many copies your book sells and the revenue generated. You receive 30% of revenues for sales under $2,000, and 75% for sales over $8,000. Similar to Amazon, they pay sixty days after sales are made. One caveat, your payment needs to be $50.00 or greater to receive a payment for the month. To view the complete royalty schedule follow this link http://www.babelcube.com/faq/revenue-share.

Within twelve hours of posting my books I inked deals to have five of my eBay books translated into Spanish by three different translators.

My personal thought is Babelcube is a great concept. They recently updated their user interface, but it's still hard to work with. I had a translator skip on three of my translations. Customer service later informed me the translator was sick, and was unsure when they would be able to complete the projects. To their credit Babelcube did quickly cancel the translations when I asked them to.

My two finished translations have been listed in waiting for publication status for the last three weeks. There is no indication when or where they will be published.

With that said, Babelcube is probably still worth a shot, especially if you feel your book has a good chance of selling in foreign markets.

To get started you need to sign up at http://www.babelcube.com/register/.

At the top of your home page there are four tabs – profile, books, translations, and messages.

When you click on Profile you're asked to provide all of your contact information. Fill in as much as you can. I posted my Amazon author bio, my picture, and included links to my website.

When you click on the Books section it gives you the option to Add Books. Follow the prompts and add your book details. I copied my book description and most of the other information from my Amazon book page. You can add just one book, or your entire catalog.

The Translations tab shows what offers you have received to translate your book, and a list of the translations you have in progress. Click on the book title and scroll down to the bottom of the page to get more information about your projects. This section shows a list of translations you have in progress, and names of the translators handling the project. At the bottom of the page there are three tabs – edit book, upload book material, and return.

Edit book lets you change your book description or upload a new cover. Upload book material lets you upload your book file, book description, and an author biography. Your translator will also translate your biography and book description when they prepare the book for publication. When you press Return it takes you back to your profile page.

The Messages tab holds all of your correspondence so you can send messages to your translators, and correspond back and forth with people wanting to translate your books.

The one thing I will say for Babelcube is they offer great customer service and are quick to respond to inquiries.

Create a paperback translation

Babelcube has added an exciting new feature for 2015 - Print books for your foreign translations.

What's nice is, they've made it simple to use. You don't need to know anything about publishing, formatting, or book layout to publish your paperback, just follow Babelcube's four easy steps.

To get started go to your Translations page. It's changed now to include a box labeled Paperbacks. Click on Paperbacks, and you will be taken to the first step of creating your new book.

When you click on Paperbacks the following box appears. It's titled Book File. Basically, you have the option of using the interior file that Babelcube generated for your book, or uploading one of your own.

You can view the file generated by Babelcube by clicking the blue link labeled here. When you do this it downloads a PDF file of your book's content. The nice thing is, Babelcube has done all of the work for you. They've formatted the text, added page numbers, and headers with your name and the title. I did a quick look through all of my books, and the page breaks are fine.

The only fault I can find is they chose to go with a 5 x 8 sizing for the books, rather than the standard 6 x 9 size for a trade paperback. It's not a big deal, and if most of the books they publish are fiction, it makes sense, because most novels are 5 x 8.

At the bottom of this page you need to choose whether you are going to use the book file provided by Babelcube, or if you prefer to upload your own.

The next section is labeled Book Properties. It lets you choose the page and cover styles for your book, Page style is a personal preference, white or cream. I prefer cream because it looks more like a regular book you can pick up at the book store. If you want a more professional look, or have numerous illustrations, white pages may be a better choice.

The next choice is whether you would like a matte or glossy cover. What that means is a dull finish (matte) or a shiny finish (glossy).My personal preference is matte, especially if the book uses dark colors like black, navy blue, or green.

The other key take away from this page is the book size - 5 x 8 inches.

Step 3 is for you to upload your Book Cover.

If you've never formatted a paperback book before, this is the trickiest step. The cover needs to be sized based on the number of pages and the page style. When it is done properly, the cover wraps around the pages for a perfect fit. If you want the book title and your name on the spine your book needs to be roughly 123 pages. If it is less than that the spine should be left blank.

I would recommend having your cover designer format the cover. That way you're guaranteed a perfect fit, and a great looking layout.

I have my covers made by a designer on Fiverr.

It's simple, inexpensive, and it's sized perfectly every time. All I have to do is send them the front cover design (normally the same one I use for my book on Babelcube), a copy of the blurb (back cover text), and a few notes about the size and formatting. I give them the book size (5 x 8), number of pages, and the page style (white or cream). The designer takes it from there, and turns it into a publishable cover.

If you prefer to do it yourself, Babelcube has a template you can download to help size and design your own cover.

The final step is to set your price, or Book Price as it is labeled by Babelcube.

This step shows you the cost of printing your book, the minimum price you are required to set for your book, and then it has a box for your to enter your price. The really cool thing is - when you enter the price, your expected royalty is shown below the price box. This gives you a chance to see how much you will make at different prices.

As soon as you're happy with your price and expected royalties, click Final Step: Publish Paperback, and the presses will start whirling.

Turning your book into a paperback really is that easy. Visit Babelcube today, and give it a shot.

Smashwords

I have a love hate affair with Smashwords. Here's the link to visit their website - https://www.smashwords.com/.

I'm happy for the opportunity to get my books on all of the sites they support, but I can't for the life of me figure out how to configure a manuscript to get it through their "meatgrinder." The good news is I don't have to. After a week of pulling out my hair and fighting urges to smash my laptop against the wall I found a guy on Fiverr who'll do all the work for me for five bucks. His Fiverr id is Bookaholic, and he does the job in three days or less. If you want to check out his gig here's the link

http://www.fiverr.com/bookaholic/format-your-ebook-for-smashwords-to-pass-autovetter.

Here's the least you need to know about Smashwords. They're a third party aggregator that posts content on their own website, and on other eBook sites. Some of the sites they make your books available on include: Amazon, Apple, Baker & Taylor, Blio, Baker-Taylor Axis 360, Barnes & Noble, Flipkart, Kobo, Page Foundry, Scribd, and Library Direct.

The big three are Apple, Kobo, and Barnes & Noble.

Apple is the toughest nut for independent authors to crack on their own because they require you to use their own eBook authoring software that only runs on – you guessed it – an Apple computer.

Publishing your book

Smashwords does all of the heavy lifting for you. When you submit a manuscript to them it gets run through their "meatgrinder." This is what converts your manuscript into all the different formats they need to publish your book on other sites. In order to do this they have very specific guidelines your manuscript needs to conform to.

For the sake of my own sanity and this book I'm not going to cover their exact requirements. I suggest using the Fiverr gig by Bookaholic. If you want to go it on your own you should check out the Smashwords Style Guide by Mark Coker. You can get your free copy here. http://www.smashwords.com/books/view/52.

Your cover art may also need some minor tweaking to work with Smashwords. They require your cover to be a minimum of 1400 pixels wide, with a height greater than the width. You can resize your cover using paint, or ask your designer to redo it for you.

Once you have your manuscript and cover ready publishing on Smashwords is easy. Click on publish in the author dashboard. Most everything is self-explanatory. The pricing and sampling section is different than on Amazon. You have the option to make your book permanently free on Smashwords. To do this select make my book free. Authors generally do this when they want to make their book permanently free on Amazon or other eBook sites. You're also given the option to let my readers determine the price. If you're feeling lucky give this one a try. Readers can pay whatever they think your book is worth. Keep in mind, if you use this option, Barnes and Noble won't publish your book if you submit it through Smashwords. The final option is charge a specific price for my book. Use this section to set the price you want for your book.

The section immediately after this lets you to set up sampling. Amazon automatically sets sampling or the look inside feature to ten percent. Smashwords lets you select the sample size for your book. Twenty percent is the default setting. They suggest fifteen percent for full size books and thirty percent for short stories. Choose the preview amount you're comfortable giving away.

Section 5 lets you select the eBook formats to make your book available in. By default all of the formats are selected. My suggestion is to leave it like that.

After you've completed all of the steps, select yes, I agree in Section 8 and Smashwords will begin to process your book.

Once you select yes, I agree your book goes into a queue waiting to be processed. When processing is completed you receive an email saying congratulations your book passed the vetting process, or you will receive a message that your book had issues going through the autovetter. If you had autovetter issues you can correct them, and resubmit your manuscript.

As soon as you receive the congratulations message your book goes on sale on the Smashwords site. It also goes into review for premium distribution, which means it is good to be sold on other sites like Apple, Kobo, and Scribd. Most often it takes about a week to review your book and get it set up for premium distribution. You can check the progress in your dashboard. The second to the last column at the far right of each book summary shows the premium status. When your book has been accepted it will show premium approved, and the date of approval. If there is an issue getting approved, you will be able to see the error code in the next column – retailer tickets. As soon as you correct the error you can resubmit your book.

Selecting distribution channels

After you submit your book you have one last task to complete, you need to select your distribution channels. To do this select channel manager in the box labeled Marketing & Distribution Tools.

When you click into the channel manager the first thing you see is an explanation of the royalties paid selling your book on the different sites. To select your sales channels scroll further down the page until you see your first book cover. Smashwords shows you the different channels available and gives you the option to Distribute or Opt Out of each channel.

I list my books on Amazon and Barnes & Noble for myself so I chose to opt out of those two programs. This way I receive payment directly from both sites and don't have to pay a commission on those sales to Smashwords. Others authors prefer the convenience of doing it all through Smashwords and just having one distributor.

After you've selected your channels to sell on it normally takes anywhere from one to four weeks for your books to start selling on those sites.

Payment

The downside of Smashwords is payments are made quarterly. Authors can choose to receive payment by PayPal, or check. The payment threshold for PayPal is $10.00, for checks the payment threshold is $75.00.

Payment dates are:

- January 31st (for sales in October, November, and December)
- April 30th (for sales in January, February, and March)
- July 31st (for sales in April, May, and June)
- October 31st (for sales in July, August, and September)

To check out Smashwords FAQs click this link –

http://www.smashwords.com/about/supportfaq#Royalties

Draft2Digital

Draft2Digital is quickly becoming my favorite publishing site. It's similar to Smashwords, but easier to use—because you don't have to fight the *meatgrinder*. You can add your books to Apple, Barnes & Noble, Kobo, Oyster, Scribd, and more, using the same *Word* file you uploaded to Amazon.

If you've never visited Draft2Digital before, click on this link - https://www.draft2digital.com/.

At the top of the page you will see four navigation tabs—My Reports, My Account, Support, and My Books.

My Books is where you add and edit books. When you click on My books, Add New Book appears at the top of the page, followed by a list of the books you currently have published through Draft2Digital.

Click on [Add New Book] to get started. The first section that pops up is edit book. This section is where you upload your book file, set your author name, add your description, keywords, and choose a category. It is intuitive and easy to use. Key takeaways are you get five keywords, and you can choose up to five categories.

After you enter all of your information, select [save and continue] at the bottom of the page.

Section two is titled [edit book layout]. At the top of the page you can upload your book cover. Below that, you are shown the extracted chapter headings from your book. What I like about this section is it breaks out your chapters into four separate categories—Introductory pages, Promotional pages, Biographical pages, and Chapter layout. It gives you a different view of your book, and allows you to see it from a reader's perspective. Does the layout make sense? Is there too much promotional material? Did you forget your author bio? And, finally—do your chapters follow a logical sequence that tell readers what your book is about and where it's going?

Select [save and continue] when you are finished.

The next section—Preview Book Layout, allows you to look at your content in three different formats—MOBI, ePUB, and PDF. Be sure to download each format, so you can check your book for formatting errors. When you're satisfied everything looks okay, place a check in the [I have reviewed this manuscript] box.

When you're happy with everything select [next] to move on to the next section.

The Publishing section is where you set your prices. First you set your price, and then you choose the venues you want to sell your book on. At this time (10/09/2015) the choices are—Nook, Kobo, iBooks, Scribd, Page Foundry, Toltino, and Oystr (shuttering up their doors soon). The royalty you will earn for each sale is displayed by the site name. At the top of the page under where you enter your book's price you have the opportunity to set territorial prices. So if you want to charge more in the UK, Canada, etc.—you can set a different price.

Click [submit] at the bottom of the page, and your almost done. On the last page you confirm your publishing rights, then select [Publish My Book].

In twelve to forty-eight hours your book will be published on the various sites.

The next tab [My Reports] is a quick summary of your sales. It shows how many books you've sold on the platform altogether, how many books you've sold this month, the previous month, and your anticipated royalties for this month and last month.

Off to the left hand side, you will see [My Reports]. It's a quick summary of your account. Under charts you can look at what's popular—sales by book so far this month, sales by book so far today, sales by contributor (if you write using pen names), royalties by sales channel, and royalties by month so far this year.

Statements allows you to download reports, tax forms, raw sales data, and your account ledger. Probably the most useful tool here is the account ledger. It gives a quick over view of royalty amounts by sales channel month over month. For me the top three sellers are iBooks, Oystr, and Barnes & Noble. If I'm lucky, the other sites pay me enough to buy a soda every third or fourth month. With Oystr shuttering its doors soon, hopefully the other sites will pick up the slack.

The [My Account] tab lets you set up various options for your account—name, formatting options, payment methods, etc.

Support is just what it says. It contains a knowledge base, FAQs, and contact hours and methods.

My suggestion is post your books to Amazon yourself so you earn the full royalty there. Use Draft2Digital or Smashwords to broadcast your books out to other sites. It will save you time, money, and frustration.

Barnes & Noble

If you're already publishing your books on Amazon, listing your books on Barnes & Noble is going to be an easy transition. To get started selling on Barnes & Noble you can follow this link https://www.nookpress.com/. Their self-publishing site is called Nook Press.

When I'm listing a new book I normally keep both sites open and cut and paste the required information from Amazon into Barnes & Noble.

To list your book, click on Create new project. You're asked to give your project a name. It can be the name of your book or another name you want to assign to it. The next screen that pops up asks you to upload your manuscript. You can use the same MS Word file you submitted to Amazon, just be sure to remove any references or links to Amazon in it.

Once your manuscript has been uploaded, click on cover image to upload your book cover.

After your cover has been uploaded you want to click on title & description. The first step is to update your title. Next you are given the option to include a publisher name. If you have your own imprint name put it here. If you don't have your own publisher name leave this item blank.

Use contributors to include anyone who participated in creating your book – authors, co-authors, editors, illustrators, etc. Below that is a section for your book description. I paste mine in direct from Amazon. The next section lets you enter your author bio. Once again, I paste it directly from Amazon.

The last question asks if you have an eBook specific ISBN. In most cases your answer will be no, and they will assign a free ISBN for your book. Be sure to click save and next at the top before you proceed, or you may lose all of your information.

After this you add categories. Barnes & Noble lets you select up to five categories, compared to only two with Kindle. Use all five categories if possible. Below this you are asked to enter keywords readers can search on to find your book. You are allowed 100 characters, and should separate each search term with a comma. At the bottom of this section you are asked to choose the appropriate audience for your book and the language your book is written in. Once again click on save and next at the top of the page.

The next page asks for information on rights and pricing. Depending upon the rights you own select World sales rights or United States only. DRM lets you choose whether you want DRM encryption set up for your book. Finally, select your list price for the United States and the United Kingdom. When you are done entering this information click save and next.

The next section concerns book details. Answer these questions, and click on save and next.

The final section allows you to enter editorial reviews. If you have some enter them here. If not click on save, and the publish button will turn green at the top. Click on it, and your book is ready to be published. One more screen pops up and asks you which version of your manuscript to use. The one you edited in the previewer (if you changed anything), or the original version you uploaded.

After this, your book should be available for sale within eight to twelve hours.

Royalties and Payments

Barnes and Noble pay out royalties sixty days after they are earned. My experience is they are not as consistent with their payouts as Amazon. Some months the payment does not arrive until two or three days into the new month, so some months you won't receive a payment.

Royalties are 40 percent for books priced under $2.98 or over $10.00. Royalties are sixty-five percent for books priced between $2.99 and $9.99.

Barnes & Noble debuted a new print on demand service today as part of its Nook Press.

From what I can see, the prices are going to be more reasonable than Lulu. I created a 180 page hardbound edition with a dust jacket for $10.10. The same book with Lulu would cost $13.25, so you save a little over $3.00 per copy. Not bad. From what I can see, you're able to order between one and 125 copies. Shipping was reasonable. I ordered two copies, and postage was $6.00.

Now for the downside. At the current time, Nook is strictly a print on demand service. They do not distribute your books, or sell them on their platform. Because of that you need to have your own method for distributing your book.

You could sell them to friends, at book signings, and on your website. You can also sell them on Amazon if you have a seller account. I did that with a few hardbacks I printed on Lulu before Amazon picked them up.

Creating the book was fairly easy once I figured out how to embed fonts in my files. The good thing is Nook Press walks you through the entire process, and explains how to embed fonts, and create PDF print ready files.

To get started you need three PDF files. The inside file, the front cover, and the back cover. Nook specifies page sizes and margins for everything so it's easy to follow along. You upload each file separately, and then create your spine.

Like I said, I ordered two copies. It sounds like it should take a week or two to receive them. I'll share the results here when I receive them.

Kobo

Kobo is the easiest to use self-publishing site I've ever come across. You can access the site by following this link. http://www.kobo.com/writinglife

To read the Kobo user manual, click on this link. http://download.kobobooks.com/writinglife/Kobo/en-US/KWL-User-Guide.pdf

As soon as you sign into Kobo you will be taken to your seller dashboard. The dashboard is the money center of Kobo. It shows you how many eBooks you've sold, and your estimated earnings.

At the top of this page, just below where it says Kobo you'll see three tabs – dashboard, eBooks, and learning center. As we already talked about, dashboard highlights your sales and earnings. eBooks is where you set up new books for publication, and the learning center is where you turn for more help in listing your books and increasing sales on Kobo.

To list your first book with Kobo, click on eBooks at the top of the page.

Select the green tab that says create new book. Listing your book is broken down into five steps.

1. Describe your eBook
2. Add eBook content
3. Choose content rights

4. Set the price
5. Publish your eBook

The form is intuitive and easy to use.

Fill in your title, subtitle, and series name if your book is part of a series. Under author, list your name, or the pen name you write under. The great thing is Kobo sets up a separate section with the books published under each author name, so you can keep your books separated by each pen name you write under.

If you have your own publisher name or imprint you can list it. Towards the middle of the page there's a section where you can list your ISBN number if you have one, otherwise leave it blank and Kobo will assign an identifier for your book.

Across from the ISBN information, there's a spot where you can add categories for your book. Kobo lets you select three categories. Try to use all three of them.

At the very bottom of the page you enter your synopsis or book description. Kobo doesn't allow you to use HTML, but they do have a formatting tool similar to MS Word where you can bold or italicize content. There's also a tool to add bullet points or line numbering to your description.

Moving back up towards the top of the page, click on the cover box to upload your cover image.

Click next to move to the section labeled Add eBook content. This is where you upload your book file. Kobo accepts your manuscript in the following formats – .epub, .doc, .docx, mobi, and .odt. After you upload your book file you can check it out by selecting download and preview this eBook. If everything looks good, click on next to move to the next section.

Choose content rights lets you select your book rights. Digital Rights Management (DRM) protects your book from copying and pirating. Geographic rights helps Kobo determine where you have legal rights to sell your book.

Click on Save and next to move to the next section. This is where you set your prices. To receive the 70 percent royalty you need to price your book between $1.99 and $12.99 in U S Dollars. If you price your book under $1.99, or over $12.99 you will receive a 45 percent royalty. As you set your prices, Kobo shows the royalty percentage and dollar amount in the two far right columns. You can set all of your geographic prices based on the U S price, or you can set a separate price for each geographic area.

This section also lets you set special promotional prices. Click on Select promo price, and it brings up a new section to set up your promo prices. First off, you need to select the special promo price, and then choose the start and end dates for your promo. You can set up your special in all territories, or choose just one geographic area for your promo.

After you've finished setting up your pricing, click Save and next. This takes you to the final section where you publish your book. You can select the date you want your book to go live, or just click the green Publish button and your book will go on sale as soon as Kobo finishes reviewing your book (normally 12 to 24 hours).

If you need to edit your book or change prices, go to the section labeled eBooks, and select the book you want to change. Make your changes, and when you're finished click publish. Most changes filter through the system in under an hour, but it can take twelve hours or more.

I've been selling on Kobo for just over a year now, and my sales are lackluster at best. I still haven't received a royalty payment. I've heard people say their sales were good, especially in Canada. I will keep updating this as time goes by, and sales start rolling in. I've also heard erotica sells extremely well on Kobo, so if that's your genre—give it a shot.

To receive a 70 percent royalty you need to price your book between $1.99 and $12.99 in U S Dollars. If you price below $1.99, or over $12.99 you receive a 45 percent royalty. That's ten percent higher than you get from Amazon for pricing books outside of their sweet spot. If you have a paperback version of your book, Kobo requires you to price the Kobo version at least 20 percent lower than the physical copy to receive their maximum royalty payment.

One other thing to keep in mind is Kobo deducts taxes from your royalties when books are sold in European countries. They take 20 percent for the VAT tax in Great Britain, and 3 percent for the VAT tax in countries within the European Union. As a result, it is suggested you mark your prices up by this amount when selling in these countries. The Kobo Writing Life User Guide has more complete information on this.

Royalty payments are paid out monthly if your royalties are over $100 for the month. If you don't reach the $100 level in a six month period, they will pay out what you have earned up to that point. Funds are deposited directly into the bank account you placed on file when signing up.

Lulu

Lulu is similar to Amazon. It's a self-publishing platform and a marketplace for eBooks and physical books. Authors have the choice of uploading eBooks, paperbacks, or hardback books, and making them available exclusively on Lulu or on other platforms

The reason I decided to publish on Lulu is they offer an easy and relatively inexpensive method for making your books available in hardback.

My original plan was to do a Kickstarter campaign to launch a new book, and use a special hardbound series as a premium giveaway for larger donations. In the meantime I made six of my books available in hardback. When you select the globalREACH retail distribution plan with Lulu it makes your books available through Ingram, Amazon, Barnes and Noble, and other online book stores.

The real problem when you go to publish a hardbound book is price.

My bestselling book is *eBay 2014*. It has 122 pages. If I price it at $49.95, my royalties are $10.11. If I price it at $39.99 my royalties are $6.11. If I set it at Lulu's absolute minimum price of $24.68 I don't make any royalties when it is sold through globalREACH distribution. If I sell the book for $49.95 on Lulu I make $27.97—not too shabby. I can also offer different discounts to buyers who purchase the book on Lulu. For example if I offer a 20 percent discount, the book would sell for $39.95, and my royalty would be $17.97. That's still not too bad, if I were to make any sales on Lulu. But, that hasn't happened.

The same book in paperback on Amazon sells regularly for $15.99, and brings me a royalty of $7.33.

So why publish your book in hardback, if you're not doing it for money? Personal satisfaction was a driving force for me to release my books in a hardbound edition. I'm old school. Readers from my generation didn't consider a book to be a real book unless it was published in a hardbound edition. When I was a kid and my favorite books came out I'd grab them in the book club edition, or wait that long six months or a year for the paperback release. (Yeah! I really am that old.)

You may have an entirely different reason for wanting to produce a hardbound copy of your book. Whatever your reason, Lulu offers print-on-demand hardcover books at prices any author can afford. If you want, you can buy a single copy. I purchased proof copies of my books for $13.00 to $15.00 each, plus shipping. At this price most authors can afford to buy a copy for mom, dad, close friends, and maybe even a few extra copies to impress reviewers. I even considered ordering five or ten extra copies to send into Amazon to sell through their FBA program. I could price them at $35.00 each, and still make a little over $10.00 a copy.

Publishing Your Book on Lulu

Lulu has an option on the front page of their website labeled *publish books for free*. Select it to get started making your book.

After this you are shown several formats available for you to produce your book in as well as sample costs and royalties for each type of book. Once you decide on the type of book you want to create, choose *Make Book* or *Make eBook* at the bottom of the page.

The next step is to select the type of book you want to make. Click on the one that corresponds to the book you want to make.

The next screen collects basic information about your book—title, author, and distribution methods. (You can make your book available to the world, or make it available just to you. The choice is yours.) After this you choose an ISBN. My suggestion is to choose a free ISBN from Lulu, otherwise you can add an ISBN you already own, or choose to proceed without an ISBN. If you assign an ISBN number to your book, be sure to write it down. If you want to make your book available through Lulu's globalREACH program you are required to add the book's ISBN number to the copyright page in a certain format. If you do this incorrectly you will have to reformat the book, and order another sample.

After this you upload your book files.

If you had your book formatted for a 6 x 9 Create Space paperback you can upload the same file to Lulu. It will have the proper formatting for their standard hardbound and paperback books. If your book hasn't been properly formatted, you will need to format it to the proper size. The easiest way to do this is to create a MS Word file, or hire a formatter on Fiverr to do it for you. Lulu has professional formatting options available too, but they will cost you much more than having it done on Fiverr.

Lulu accepts your book in a number of different formats including PDF, Doc, Docx, and others. After you upload it, you need to select *Make Print Ready File* on the next page. This creates the file Lulu will use to make your book. You are given the option to preview it so you can check for formatting errors.

When you are happy with your book file select *Save and Continue*. This will take you to the section where you create the dust jacket for your book.

If you're just looking for a basic dust jacket, you can design it yourself using Lulu's book cover creator. Pictures are uploaded in the tray on the right side of the page. After that you can drag and drop them into the appropriate spaces on your dust jacket. To add text, click on the white text tabs and type in your blurbs.

If you're looking for a more professional design I would suggest hiring an experienced designer on Fiverr or Elance.

The next page lets you preview your cover. When you're happy with it select *Make Print-Ready Cover* at the bottom of the page.

When you're finished creating your book cover Lulu asks you to describe your project. First you need to select a category. You're only allowed to pick one, so choose the most appropriate category for your book. Next you need to add the keywords readers will search for on Lulu to find your book. Be sure to separate each keyword phrase with a comma. Your description needs to be between 50 and 1,000 characters, so if you are copying your description from Amazon you may have to cut it down a bit. The rest of the fields are pretty self-explanatory—language, copyright info, license, edition, and publisher. The only field that could be tricky is license. If you're in doubt choose, *Standard Copyright License*.

Now you set your project price. You can play around with it a little until you find a price you think is right. The form shows you how much you will make at each retail price if your book sells on Lulu, or with globalREACH distribution. You can also set a discount for sales on Lulu. This lowers your royalties, but can make your books more attractive to buyers.

The final step is to review the information you entered for your book. Everything is presented on a review page. If you need to change something, select edit and make your changes. If everything looks good, give the go ahead to publish your book.

At this point your book is for sale to buyers on Lulu.

If you want to make your book available through globalREACH distribution where it is available through Ingram, Amazon, Barnes and Noble, and other distributors you have to jump a few more hurdles. First you need to purchase a sample copy of the book. After you receive your sample you need to return to your My Projects page to approve it. If you make any changes to your book after reviewing the sample copy you need to order another proof and then approve it.

Sales wise, there's not much I can tell you. I've made maybe two hundred bucks over the last two years selling on Lulu. But remember, most of the books I created are hardbound editions that retail for $49.95 each. The story might be different if I had created lower priced paperback books or eBooks.

Experiment for yourself to decide if a hardbound edition is on tap for one of your books. And, if you're like me—there's something about being able to hand someone a hardbound copy of your book. It's more substantial. It's a symbol that you've made it. You're a writer!

Google Play & Google Books

Google Play and Google Books offer another option for authors to sell their books.

Google Books is the world's largest repository of out-of-print and current books. Readers can search through millions of books looking for information on a particular subject, and Google Books will show them the pages in your book that contain the search terms they are looking for. Every day readers, researchers, and authors turn to Google Books to find answers to their research questions.

Having your book listed on Google Books can open it up to an entirely new audience.

Google Play is Google's version of Kindle or the iStore. They deliver books to readers who use their Android based platform. You can check out Google Play here https://play.google.com/store.

Getting started

To get started listing your books on Google go to https://play.google.com/books/publish/. If you're not signed up for the Google Partners Program you will need to sign up for it first.

At the top of the browser page it says Google Play in the upper left corner. Below that you will see four tabs – Book

Catalog, Analytics & Reports, Payment Center, and Account Settings.

Book Catalog is where you add new books. Select the Add Books tab, and follow the prompts. A pop up screen will ask you for a book identifier (ISBN). Type in your book's ISBN. If it doesn't have an ISBN click on the box below that. Click ok, and you will be taken to the next screen.

If Google can locate your book in its database it prepopulates all of the screens with the information available. If Google doesn't find your book you will need to fill in all of the information. Where it asks for a biographical note, I paste in my Amazon author bio. Below that is a section labeled subjects. Use it to add categories for your book. Age groups lets you target different groups your book will appeal to. If the description doesn't prepopulate, copy and paste it from Amazon. When you are done filling in all of the info, click on save at the top of the page.

Click on Google Play Settings in the left hand column. The first thing you're asked is to add a new price. Click on Add a new price. Type in the currency your book is priced in (For example US Dollars is USD). In the next box you need to type in the price (example 3.99). Finally, you're asked to choose the location for that price. To make it easy, use "World." If you have different prices for different locations, you would need to add each of them separately. Follow through the rest of the prompts on this page. If you are unsure how to answer hover your mouse over the question mark and it will guide you through answering the question. Click on save at the top of the page.

Click on Google Book Settings in the left hand column. The first question asks you to select the preview type, or the percentage of your book you want to make available to readers. Twenty percent is the default, or you can choose another preview amount from twenty to one hundred percent. If you have the book available for sale directly from your website, fill in the buy link text and buy link, otherwise leave these lines blank. The publisher link is the link to your publisher website if you have one, otherwise leave this line blank. You can also upload a publisher logo if desired. Click on save at the top of the page.

Click on Content Files in the left hand column. This is where you upload your book files. Your book file needs to be uploaded in PDF or epub formats. The cover should be uploaded as a JPEG. At the bottom of this page you have the option to upload a list of Quality Reviewers. To add someone as a quality reviewer they must have a Google account. Click on add, and enter their email address. Click ok, and continue doing this to add more reviewers. When you are finished click the save button at the top of the page. Your quality reviewers will be able to access your book on their PCs or on their reading devices.

Reports / Payment Center / Account Settings

I want to briefly outline the other three selections you see under Google Play in the far left column of your screen.

Analytics and reports lets you pull up reports regarding your book traffic and sales. The most irritating thing about Google is they don't provide a sales dashboard where you can quickly review your sales and earnings. Each time you want to check sales you need to generate a new report and download it as an Excel spreadsheet. Can you say irritating? Hopefully the folks at Google will figure this one out and make it more user friendly.

The information in payment center needs to be completed before your books can go live on Google Play and Google Books. To get started, click on the payment center tab. Click on Add Payment profile. Give your payment profile a name, and fill in the information asked for – name, address, etc.

The first thing you need to do is set up your payment settings. By default you are set up to receive monthly payments with a $1.00

payment threshold. You can change your payment threshold to another dollar amount, or you can have Google hold your payments for a specified period (up to one year). After you've completed this step, click on Add new bank account. Before you can finish setting up your bank account you need to wait for Google to make a test deposit to your account. When you see the deposit has been made to your account, click on Add new bank account again to verify the deposit amount.

Next you need to click on billing profile. Click on edit, and scroll down to tax profile. Enter your tax information in the online W9 form.

Scroll down to sales territories. Click on add a territory. Select a payment profile from the drop down menu. In the choose territories section most often you will type in "world." If you only hold rights in certain areas, click on the question mark and it will tell you how to set up individual territories. If you're subject to fixed pricing laws in any of the countries put a check mark in the box. If not, leave this box blank. Click on enable this region configuration, and select create territory.

The final section is Account Settings. Use it to ensure your contact information is correct, or to make any changes.

From signing up to verifying my account to listing my first books it took about seven days for my books to begin showing up in Google Play and Google Books.

Royalty rates and payments

I couldn't find any mention of royalties in the Google Play FAQs. When I searched for it in their help section it said there were no help pages for that topic. I don't know about anybody else, but that sort of scares me.

FYI: I sold my first book on Google Play three days after it went live. I set my list price at $4.99. Google discounted it to $3.60. They paid an after tax royalty based on a $3.00 selling price, so my royalty worked out to $1.56, or 52 percent. Lesson learned: Add at least $2.00 to your selling price to ensure you receive the royalty you were expecting. The end result is I made fifty cents less than I would have received selling the same book for $2.99 on Amazon.

The good news is Google pays thirty days after sales are made, not sixty days like Amazon and Barnes and Noble so you will receive your payments sooner. And, they pay at the beginning of the month, not at the end of the month like all other e-publishers.

Final Wrap up

In the immortal words of the Looney Tunes, "That's all folks!"

Thank you for hanging in there until the end. I know it's been a long ride. Hopefully you've learned a few things to make self-publishing your book easier and more profitable.

If I could give you just one piece of advice, it would be to hang in there and keep writing.

Sometimes an author gets lucky, and their first book takes off, and starts selling like hot cakes from the get-go, but most times it's a slow process. You publish a book to Kindle, or Smashwords, check back to your sales dashboard every few hours, and nothing – Nothing at all happens.

A week goes by, and you sell one, or two books. Another week, and two, or three more sales trail in. Maybe mom finally bought a copy, or maybe an old school mate in Davenport, or Clinton (hint!) heard about your book, and decided to give it a read.

The fact is building an audience takes time. Building an audience that really likes your books takes even longer.

The best advice I can give you is to write your book. Spend a few days promoting it. Start writing another book, and repeat the process. Over time you will sell more books.

When I was a full time eBay seller I had good weeks and bad weeks. I couldn't really do anything to make the bad weeks better.

All I knew was if I continued to do the right stuff, (post more listings and offer exceptional customer service), more sales would follow. Writing, and self-publishing, is a lot like that.

Keep writing. Make your books available in as many formats as possible – eBooks, paperbacks, and audio books.

If you write nonfiction, keep updating your older books, and make sure they're current. Publish new editions every year or so.

You never know what's going to happen. I have books that never sold over ten copies on Kindle, and out of the blue someone orders fifty or a hundred copies in paperback. As soon as I added audio books to the puzzle, they began selling hundreds of copies per month.

It's crazy, but true. If you publish enough books – You just might become an overnight sensation after enough people stumble across your books.

Keep writing…

Nick Vulich

Read these books next

My original idea was to write a book titled *57 Must Read Books for Kindle Publishers*. Over time it morphed into my blog, *indie author's toolbox*, and then this book.

I've read just about every book written about Kindle, self-publishing, and e-course creation. Many of them have been helpful; a few have raised more questions than they answered. I finally narrowed my recommended reading list down to these ten books.

I only chose one book by Steve Scott, but any of his books would be a good starting point for authors new to self-publishing. I picked on Tom Corson-Knowles in the first section of this book for not keeping *Ninja Book Marketing Strategies* up-to-date, but truth be told, Tom does know his stuff, and you would do well to read any of his books.

If you're new to the writing game any of Rob Parnell's *The Easy Way to Write* guides would be enlightening. Rob's a great guy who's passionate about helping writer's improve their skills. While you're at it, you might want to check out his wife's book. It's called, *Show Don't Tell, The Ultimate Writer's Guide.* Her name is Robyn Opie Parnell, and her book is an excellent primer that explains how to bring your writing to life.

Martin Crosbie is another author who took time out to share tidbits of his self-publishing journey with me. Martin is a novelist, and the author of *How I Sold 30,000 eBooks on Amazon's Kindle.* Martin is on a mission to help other writers, and it shines through in his blog, his books, and every action he takes.

My special thanks go out to Norm Schriever. He was the first of many interviews for my blog. I caught up with Norm while he was traveling through Southeast Asia researching his newest book. His book, *The Book Marketing Bible* has a lot of great tips and tricks for self-publishers.

Finally, I want to thank the dynamic duo of Buck Flogging – Matt Stone and Rob Archangel. Their book *Kill Your Blog* got me started contacting other authors to pick their brains, and discover what makes them tick. Here's the magical advice, direct from their book, "email somebody. Send them a direct message on Facebook. Call those fools."

Now I ask you, what could be more inspiring than that? Who would have figured all I had to do was shoot someone an email, and they'd drop everything to help me out.

Here's to all of the authors who take time out to help the newbies along the way.

As Mr. Spock would say, "May you live long, and prosper."

Writing Habit Mastery by S. J. Scott (alias Steve Scott). Time management, and motivation, or the lack of them, seem to be two of the biggest stumbling blocks facing new authors. This book gives a lot of great practical advice to get you writing, and keep you cranking out book after book.

What amazes me about Steve is he's totally transparent in all of his books and blog posts. The one thing he always talks about is giving readers value for the money they invest in his books. Other writers talk about price pulsing, and earning the most money possible from each of their books. Steve is always out there pitching his books at 99¢, $2.99, or free. And, the thing is, when you hear him talk about his numbers this strategy has paid off better over the long haul than higher prices ever would have.

The Art of Story: Writing Fiction that Sells by Rob Parnell. Rob is a novelist who has made his mark creating writing guides to help new authors hone their craft. I know he's most proud of his newest book, *The Writer and the Hero's Journey*, but I think this one would be a good entry point for anyone looking to explore his guides. The best part of these books is Rob starts with the basics and helps you outline your book as you learn.

I interviewed Rob awhile back, and his desire to teach new writers filtered through everything he had to say. Talking about new writers, he said "My view is that if you're finding writing difficult, you're probably not doing it right! New authors need to relax and stop being so hard on themselves."

One other tip I got from Rob was, "We need to get past the words – and really get to grips with what we're trying to describe effectively. It's a process of undoing what we're taught. I guess that's why it seems like a difficult process. The best advice is to just write more – and try not to think too hard about the words. Concentrate on feelings, images, and ideas first, and then write quickly."

Write. Publish. Repeat. By Sean Platt and Johnnie B. Truant. Hands down this is one of the best books about self-publishing. These guys hit on every topic, from content creation and writing, to publishing, and marketing. Key-takeaways are to concentrate on finding your true fans, so they can spread the word about your books.

And, just like the title says: write, publish, and repeat. Putting more content out there is one sure way to help you get discovered.

Let's Get Visible by David Gaughran. This book is filled with great advice on how to get your book noticed such as – how to battle the "sales cliff" – that point where your book stalls out, and getting new sales seems more difficult than pulling teeth. There's a great section that explains Amazon algorithms so you can better understand what it takes to get the power of Amazon behind your book. Another section details pricing, and price pulsing (where you vary prices to optimize your books sales and profits).

Goodreads for Authors: How to Use Goodreads to Promote Your Books by Michelle Campbell-Scott. Goodreads is a great way to promote your book. More so for novelists than for nonfiction writers, but it's also challenging to get started.

Perhaps the most difficult thing to understand is Goodreads reviews. If you're used to receiving mostly 5 star reviews on Amazon, Goodreads is going to burst your bubble. A 5 star review on Amazon translates in to 3 or 4 stars on Goodreads, just because of the way they define them. If you can get over the shock of that, Goodreads can be a great marketing tool for writers.

Authors can claim their author page to build a profile, add a picture, and add their blog feed. Goodreads also lets you do paperback giveaways to increase reviews and interest in your book. Read the book and discover how you can harness Goodreads to build your sales and your brand.

How I Sold 30,000 eBooks on Amazon's Kindle, An Easy-to-Follow Self-Publishing Guide by Martin Crosbie. Best piece of advice, "Everything leads to something else, and you never know who might be reading your work or watching your career." For Martin, writing books led to speaking, teaching, and writing more books. Who knows where your writing will take you. His other advice is similar to that from all successful self-publishers – you're going to need more than one book, so keep writing.

I revisited this one again last night, and I really think every author needs to spend some time with it. Martin's attitude is really remarkable. I've said it before, and I'm going to say it again—everything Martin talks about involves giving freely of yourself to help newer authors learn the trade. Each step along the way he tried new things, and reached out to help others. Each time he did this, new doors opened up for him – writing, teaching, or some other method, to help promote his books.

Like it. Hate it. It doesn't really matter. Just read it, and start giving back to move your career forward.

How to Build a Powerful Writers Platform in 90 Days by Austin Briggs. I hesitated listing this book. Not because it's a bad book, but because following the advice in it requires a major commitment of time and cash. I don't think an author platform is right for everyone, especially on the scale Briggs outlines here. I do think there's a lot of great info on creating an author website, employing social media, and building your online presence. Check it out. Follow the entire program, or pick and choose the portions you have the time and resources to implement.

Building Your Fanbase by Shannon O'Neil and Toni Tesori (duolit). Authors "have successful writing careers because they have fans, not because they have readers." Think about it for a moment. Readers don't make your career – raving fans do! So how do you find and cultivate them. That's what this book is all about – determining who your ideal fans are and catering to them. Sean Platt and Johnnie B. Truant said it in *Write. Publish. Repeat.* You only need 1,000 true fans to have a wildly successful writing career. Use this information to discover your 1,000.

Author! Author! Use Book Discounts & Promos to Create Buzz for your Book by Katherine Mariaca-Sullivan. I've never been big on doing much promotion for my KDP Free giveaways, but after reading this book, and Martin Crosbie's *How I Sold 30,000 Books on Amazon's Kindle,* I think that's probably got to change. This book has some good lists that show where to promote your book during its KDP Free run. I think any author can benefit from the ideas in this book. You may also want to visit her other book, *Author! Author! Publish & Market a Buzz-Creating How-To Book.*

How to Sell Video Courses online, How I Earn $1000+ a Month While I Sleep by Rob Cubbon. Rob's book technically isn't about writing or self-publishing, but for some writers it could lead to one of those ah-ha moments where they move beyond books to email or online courses. The book is easy to read, and a good starting point if you were thinking about online instruction.

I interviewed Rob for my blog awhile back and here's one of the tips he shared. "Turning an eBook into a course is one of the easiest things because you already have the content and the structure. Here's what you do. Condense every chapter of your Kindle into a few slides in PowerPoint or whatever application you'd like to use. Use ScreenFlow or Camtasia to film the slides while you use your book to narrate over them. It's easy to "ad lib" whilst you're reading your own text."

PS: I'm going to hold him to that promise to help me create an e-course one of these days.

There are a lot of other books out there about writing, self-publishing, and how to build a raving fan base. I owe a debt to all of them, and I'd like to apologize for not having time or space to mention them all.

Know this: Your time and effort are appreciated.

Thank-you very much!

Been there, done that

Okay, you've heard what I think. Now it's time to learn what the experts think. Each of these interviews were originally published on my blog, *Indie Author's Toolbox*. They offer some of the most progressive, and innovative information, available on self-publishing.

Steve Scott is the go-to guy for self-publishing information. Steve has written five highly successful Kindle books about writing and self-publishing. He runs the SteveScottSite, and has created a podcast to help new self-publishers.

Over the last several years Steve has developed a new Habits niche, writing as S. J. Scott. He has published several top 100 books on Amazon, including *Crowd Source Your Success, How Accountability Helps You Stick to Goals; 10-Minute Declutter, The Stress-Free Habit for Simplifying Your Home;* and *Habit Stacking 97 Small Life Changes That Take Five Minutes or Less.*

Buck Flogging is the creation of the notorious duo, Matt Stone and Rob Archangel. Buck is the super-cool genius behind *Buck Books,* a new type of Kindle Promotion site that has skyrocketed several participating authors into the top 100 on Amazon.com.

When they're not acting out their fantasies as Buck Flogging, the guys write Kindle Books, record audio books, and format books for Kindle and CreateSpace. You can check out all the services they offer at *http://archangelink.com/*.

Martin Crosbie is a novelist, and one of those authors we'd all do well to emulate. Martin gives freely of himself to everyone who asks. If you've got a question about writing or self-publishing, he will drop everything to answer, or, at least he did for me.

He teaches writing seminars, is a regular contributor to the *Indies Unlimited* blog, and is the author of *How I Sold 30,000 eBooks on Amazon's Kindle, An Easy-To-Follow Self-Publishing Guidebook 2015*.

Rob Parnell has written over 40 non-fiction self-help titles, and been published all over the world. He is a composer, singer, music producer and budding movie maker. His preferred genre is the thriller - sometimes with a supernatural edge - in which he writes short stories, graphic novels, YA novels and adult thrillers.

While this interview is not about the mechanics of self-publishing, it's on another subject, even more important—writing your masterpiece. Rob offers good, solid advice, to help improve the quality of your writing.

Nick Vulich

Interview with Steve Scott

Steve Scott

Steve Scott is a Kindle favorite in the writing, and habit categories. He has written numerous best sellers, and is considered an expert in self-publishing.

When I interviewed Matt Stone a few months ago, I asked him what it was like to work with Steve Scott, he told me "Steve is an efficiency machine." How do you respond to that?

I guess that's a good thing. Honestly, I don't think I work any harder than most people. The difference is I believe in creating schedules for writing and completing a minimum word count on a daily basis. Before I do anything else during a workday, I make sure to complete my writing. I feel that if authors applied this type of structure in their day, they could easily crank out a consistent level of content.

....

Most books about self-publishing talk about price pulsing and optimizing your book's selling price to make the most money possible. Whenever you talk about pricing, you talk about keeping your price low, and how important it is to offer your readers value for their dollar. Can you talk about that philosophy a little, and how it has paid off for you?

The mistake that I see many authors make is to squeeze the maximum amount of money on a single purchase. I believe that providing value, at a good price, is the best long-term strategy for getting repeat customers. You see, your goal shouldn't be to make a bunch of money on one book. You want to give a valuable enough reading experience that a reader will come back and buy the other books in your catalog. So while I don't make as much with an upfront purchase, I'm confident that I make more money in the long-term because single purchase readers will go on to check out (i.e. buy) other offers.

....

You've recently started making the move away from a Kindle only platform. Some of your books are available as Create Space paperbacks, and as Audible audio books. How is that move working out for you? And, do you feel it is something more Kindle publishers should be doing?

The results have been mixed. I barely make my money back on CreateSpace books, but they also show a nice "price differential" on the Kindle books, so the $2.99 price looks more attractive. The Audible stuff has been great so far. Out of five books, four have made their money back. In addition, the income is starting to creep up to the $1k to $2k range, which is a nice supplement to the Kindle books.

I feel that authors should try out both platforms--at least on their bestselling books. My advice is to try it with the books that generate at least five sales a day. Odds are it will have enough "visibility" to get traction on the new platforms.

....

You've also been more active with social media recently, posting on Facebook and SlideShare. Can you talk a little about your social media strategy, and how it's working for you?

I'm still not the best with social media. I do respond back to people on Twitter and occasionally post an article, but I never seem to have time to get on there. Facebook is the same...I'll occasionally post, but it's not a vital part of my marketing.

SlideShare is awesome so far. What I like about this platform is I can "systematize" the whole thing with my VA. Basically she takes my content and turns them into interesting looking presentations. From there, I drive most of the traffic back to a squeeze page, which helps grow my overall brand. I think there's lot of potential to SlideShare, so I'm spending the next few months trying to maximize the results.

....

Your book **Is 99 cents the New Free?** *started a trend that got a lot of authors to switch up their prices, and make a run for number one in their category using a 99 cent price point. You use a lot of different strategies to keep* *your books selling – permafree, 99 cents, KDP Free Days, and Countdown Deals.*

Could you explain your pricing strategy, and which ones work best for you?

Without a doubt, discounted my books to $0.99 has been my top strategy. I do this during a book launch where I'll start with a $0.99 for a week, then raise it $2.99. And I also use this strategy with Countdown Deals. Every 90 days, each book can have a week-long Countdown Deal. So I make sure to use this special promotion to increase my overall unit sales and get more visibility of my brand.

....

It seems to me readers are losing their patience with short books. Kindle Shorts, especially are receiving bad reviews, for being too short, or incomplete. Even the big guys like Steven King and Janet Evanovich are feeling the wrath. Do you think it's time for Kindle authors of both fiction and nonfiction to rethink the strategy of putting out short books focused on a single topic?

Don't really agree with this statement. While I do agree that many readers don't like short (like 30 pages or less) books that offer no value, I still feel there is a lot of value to writing shorter books (15,000 to 20,000 words). The key here is to tightly focus on one specific topic and make sure you're answering every possible question a reader might have.

....

What's next for Steve Scott? You made it big with your self-publishing titles. Your "Good Habits" books are doing extremely well. Do you have another niche in mind, or is there some other genre you've always wanted to write in?

Honestly, the habits books are doing so well that I'm going to continue working on growing the overall brand. Right now, I'm focused on building up my email list using various traffic strategies (social media, SlideShare, Google organic search). The idea here is to have such a large list that whenever I have a new book or Countdown Deal, I'll have an audience that's ready to check it out.

....

Let's talk about your mailing list for a minute. Do you think you would be as successful as you are if you didn't have your list? How about for a new author just getting started, how important do you think building an email list is to their success?

Not at all. I'm sure I would have sold a few books, but nowhere near as much if I didn't focus on list building from the beginning. From my testing and tracking, I've learned that email marketing is the #1 strategy for promoting Kindle books. So for new authors, I would recommend spending just as much time focusing on list building as I would writing Kindle books.

....

What do you think the next big trend in self-publishing is going to be? I mean Audible (audio books) is still a growth market. Compare their 150,000 books available to the millions on Amazon. That number has got to break a million in the next five years. How about video? Or interactive books?

I'd say that the Audible market is definitely going to grow. This is especially true if Amazon makes it as easy to download and consume content like they do with Kindle books.

....

Have you given any thought to where the markets going, or how self-publishers can stay ahead of the curve?

Ultimately it's going to get increasingly difficult to compete on the Kindle platform. There are so many authors now that are vying for the attention of readers. To stay ahead of the curve, I recommend building your own platform. Specifically you should focus the majority of your efforts on building an email list--even if that means sacrificing profits up front. The better "connection" you have with subscribers, the more books you'll sell in the long-term.

....

Last question, I promise. What do you think is the number one thing new writers can or should do to make themselves standout and be successful?

I'll give you two: (1) Find a niche where there is an actual audience full of people who experience a variety of problems that need to be solved. (2) Regularly (every 4 to 6 weeks) publish great books that each provide an in depth solution.

About Steve Scott

Steve Scott has developed two highly successful niches on Kindle. The first one on writing and publishing Kindle books and his most recent is the Good Habits Series. His newest book Habit Stacking: 97 Small Changes that Take Five Minutes or Less. It's currently trending to crack Kindle's top 100 list. You can learn more about Steve by visiting his blogs:

http://www.developgoodhabits.com/
or http://www.stevescottsite.com/.

Interview with Buck Flogging

Matt Stone

Matt Stone and Rob Archangel are cofounders of Archangels, Inc., and they've graciously agreed to share some of their knowledge about Kindle publishing.

Matt, you pulled the plug on blogging to write Kindle books. Do you have any regrets?

Matt: Dear lord no. I've added almost 100 new direct email subscribers daily since the blog went down. It's steady, too. In fact, yesterday I got exactly 100 new subscribers. It took me 7 years to get 3,500 subscribers. In the last 100 days I've gone from 3,500 to 12,600. I'm selling more books, writing much less, and everything worked out as planned. Plus, I've got way more time on my hands to do other things, which have included launching two new online ventures without hurting my first business at all.

....

You talk about how easy it was to get started on Amazon. 1) Because you had a catalog of books, and 2) You had a ready audience.

Matt: I believe the way you put it was, "Having an established audience to use as rocket fuel for a book launch is, quite simply, everything when it comes to success on Kindle."

....

What about the guy who doesn't have a catalog of books, or an audience to drive to his book? What do you think he should concentrate on starting out?

Matt: If you do the work and keep at it, it's almost a mathematical certainty that you will achieve success with a decent strategy in today's modern publishing environment. The formula is simple, create a big loop that builds upon itself with each round. Write a book, get as many free downloads as possible, use your book to drive subscriptions back on your website, then price it low and let it sell some copies. Repeat this process again and again. With each round your mailing list will grow, each free promotion will sell other books in your collection, and the amount of download activity you generate at launch will steadily push each new book release higher and higher in the ranks (as that mailing list grows). By the time you have 13 books you can run a 5-day free promotion every week and subsist on that activity almost exclusively.

How important is your mailing list to your success? Do you think you'd be where you are now, if you had just published your book and hoped for the best?

Matt: I had huge success before I had a big mailing list, but that was mostly through the connections I had made with other influencers in my niche. If you can get someone with a big audience to promote your book, that's a lot more significant than even tapping into your very own mailing list. People who already have an audience built, if you can tap into those people with radical generosity and irresistible sincerity, can help you reach success almost overnight. I just built a business successful enough to be overwhelmed with clients by the third month primarily with three emails to the right people in my appropriate niche.

Rob Archangel

Many authors look at social media as a major time suck. You take the opposite view. You say, "It's really important to focus that time on doing the stuff that works."

You suggest, "Posting good content, links to interesting stuff, great survey questions, funny pics and memes, short rants, and whatever is relevant to the subject matter you want to be known for – as well as intimately interacting with people (especially people of influence as we'll discuss in the next chapter), is the best way to build a good social media following fast."

....

Can you tell me one or two social media tactics that have worked best for you?

Matt: I communicate frequently with dozens of people with over 100,000 Facebook fans. I'm not a very gifted social media builder, because I've always been spread out so thin. But do those people have tremendous power and influence to turn everything around them to gold? Absolutely. They built their following by posting a dozen times a day with a mix of questions, pics, trending topics, videos, and other engaging content. Most of them used a virtual assistant to do this for them for $100 a week. I plan to take advantage of this soon for a new company of mine.

....

Another thing you talk about is getting rid of all your fears and phobias and just reaching out to touch people you want to meet? That's how you and Rob hooked up.

Say I want to shoot for the moon, and reach out to Stephen King and let him know I wish he'd go back to the days of writing short books, I could read in a few days. How should I contact him? What would you suggest saying?

Matt: Well, I wouldn't bother with big celebrities like ol' Steve K. There are literally hundreds of thousands of middle-class internet entrepreneurs out there that have the power to ignite your career, who are also totally approachable. You may not know them by name yet, but search around and always make a note of all the movers and shakers, big, medium, and small, in your area of expertise. You can get great tips from these people, do favors for them (not in a brown noser kind of way, but in a cool way that maintains your dignity), and build great relationships--and accelerate your success in the process. I know this sounds nebulous, but man does it ever work when done right. Help the right people, get reciprocation from powerful people, and use that to reach out to a bigger audience.

Rob: That's actually how Matt and I connected years ago. I followed his work and was moved to email him just because I liked what he had to say and he seemed like a cool dude. We communicated over email and through his website for a couple years, had a chance to meet and connect in person, and then later when he needed some help on some outreach and communication projects, he had me in mind. We started collaborating and now almost a couple of years later we're making some noise in the indie publishing world, having learned a lot together since we started.

....

Publishing my books to Create Space was a major turning point for me. I was struggling to get by until I made my catalog available in paperback. Why do you think so many authors think print is dead, and stubbornly cling to a Kindle only publishing policy?

Matt: It's worth it to publish in paperback just to get the little price strikethrough shown on your kindle listing. It also makes you look more like a real, reputable author and not some indie-publishing hack putting out 20-page books with 50 typos and second-rate content. I make more in audiobooks than paperbacks now, but paperbacks are still worth it. They make up about 20% of my total author royalties, but it's different for each author. We're helping someone publish a cookbook soon, and that will probably do much better than that in terms of kindle to paperback sales proportions.

Rob: I think indie authors discount print also in part because they know how hard it is for most authors to get on the shelves of

Barnes and Noble, unless they have one of the big publishing houses behind them, and even then, unless they're one of the big shots they get behind. There are plenty of Random House books you'll never see on the end cap of bookstore aisles.

Working on Kindle only also makes the self-publishing process easier to in-house. It's more time and effort to format a paperback yourself. You actually have to know a bit about typefaces and layout and be willing to go back and forth, making multiple proofs, to make sure everything looks the way it's supposed to. Formatting for the reflow-able text of e-readers has some of its own particularities, but in the end, I'd say it's a good bit simpler than doing the actual layout of a print book, where every decision you make translates directly to the end-user experience.

……………………..

The last thing I want to talk about is audio books. Matt, you recorded "S. M. A. R. T. Goals Made Simple" for Steve Scott. What was it like working for Steve? I've been following both series of his books for years, and he seems to have it all together.

Matt: Steve is an efficiency machine, and he knows how to examine some numbers and make a quick, smart decision. I found out about Steve back in November while researching everything I could about publishing. I emailed him three days later and had a manuscript to record a few weeks later. He now routinely has us turn all of his manuscripts into paperback and audiobook (at least a book per month), and he just promoted us on his website, landing us seven audiobook projects in the last 48 hours of when I write this. So yeah, it's good to send emails to the right people. I spent two minutes locating his email address on his website, and crafted the email in 5 minutes. I've already gotten more than $1,000 per minute out of that email. Did I mention emailing people and offering a service to them helps?

Rob: Building the right connections is everything, as Matt says. Steve is great to work with in part because, having established our thoroughness and the quality of our work, he lets us take the reins and doesn't micro-manage. Knowing that we can make the little decisions that have to be made, rather than doing everything by committee, saves both him and us time, and makes each project simple and straightforward. If I had to wait on him for feedback on the preferred indentation pattern for lists, or pagination preferences, or ideas for numbered versus lettered lists, or the particular font size for a heading versus sub-heading within a paperback, and we had to do that for every project, we'd grind to a halt, and ultimately end up producing something that would likely be no better than us doing it ourselves.

Likewise for audiobooks: did you want the emphasis on the second or third word of that sentence? How about a dramatic pause to let that idea sink in? Or maybe you want to build some momentum and speed up as you get closer to the end of the paragraph? How about some vocal variance? Where do you want that? Those sorts of decisions are best left to us.

....

What advice do you have for authors who want to publish their books on Audible?

Matt: Get it done or have it done for you, and man up for upfront payment instead of the royalty split unless you have a book that doesn't sell well and is 400 pages long. Most poorly-selling eBooks will bring in over $1,000 per year through ACX (which lists on Audible, iTunes, and Amazon) and most indie authors are publishing a lot of 15,000-word books that can be produced from scratch for just $400. It will hurt to pay up front, but over the course of years, trading hundreds for thousands is better than the traditional 50:50 author/narrator split.

Rob: And we say that as audiobook producers with more to gain from convincing you to split royalties with people like us. We still will do royalty splits and may end up doing more in the long term. But if we were committed to having your fiduciary interest at heart, flat-fee up front production would be the recommendation.

....

What types of books sell best? Are their certain genres or types of books that don't sell at all?

Matt: Fiction and self-help/motivational kind of stuff is what I'm seeing excel. One book we produced is making $1,500 per month on a book that is lucky to bring in $1,000/month on Kindle and Create Space combined. But I have publishing and health/nutrition books that I've done, and like I said, the audiobooks have ended up being more viable than paperbacks, with audiobook royalties increasing every month while paperbacks stay about the same. Don't wait to hear about how great audiobooks are selling in three years. Get in and get positioned and be on the plane as it takes off instead of diving for the wing as it taxis to the runway.

....

I was amazed by the number of offers I received when I made my books available for publication on Audible. Many of my books had five to seven auditions the same day. Is that normal?

More to the point, if there are so many people looking to voice audio books, what should an author look for when he's listening to auditions, and trying to select a voice actor?

Matt: We have no experience with that whatsoever, as we don't audition for books or get into that whole competitive madness, but get used to it. Voiceover people, especially those looking for a royalty split, are clamoring to join the party right now. The number of customers flooding Audible right now is creating a rapidly-increasing demand for audiobooks, and quick increases in sales figures.

Rob: Our niche is making audiobooks affordable for the small and mid-sized authors, who don't have thousands and thousands to shell out for Neil Gaiman to read their work. And so we've pinched every penny to keep costs low. Perhaps at some point our pricing will change to reflect our experience in the arena and to handle the increased demand. But right now, Archangel Ink is still on a rookie contract. If you're looking for someone not us, you'll want to find the right balance of 'knows what they're doing and can do a great job' and 'not yet so established in their career that you're priced out as a middle class author.

....

With all of that said, is there anything you want said about Rob or Matt, and is it ok to ask, which one of you is Buck Flogging anyway?

He is I and I am him, slim with the tilted brim, what's my flutherbucking name? Buck Floggy Flogg. The bomb.

About Buck Flogging

Matt Stone and Rob Archangel are co-founders of Archangel Ink (archangelink.com), an outfit established to help make self-publishing easy for authors. They've produced more than two dozen audiobooks and counting, design covers, format for Kindle and paperback print on demand, and serve as marketing consultants to help their authors maximize their current reach and leverage that into greater success and prominence. You can connect with them through the contact form at the main page of their website. Visit our books page at http://archangelink.com/books/.

Interview with Martin Crosbie

Martin Crosbie

Martin Crosbie is the author of *My Name Is Hardly* - Book Two of the *My Temporary Life Trilogy*, *Lies I Never Told - A Collection of Short Stories*, *How I Sold 30,000 eBooks on Amazon's Kindle - An Easy-To-Follow Self-Publishing Guidebook*, 2014 Edition, and *Believing Again: A Tale Of Two Christmases*.

The title of your book is **How I Sold 30,000 eBooks on Amazon's Kindle.** *That's a lot of books. What's it feel like to hit that number? Do you feel lucky? Blessed? Or ___ ?*

Martin: Both! I'm totally blessed to have been able to connect with so many readers, and part of that was due to being in the right place at the right time. I signed on to Amazon's KDP Select program at the end of 2011 and my timing was perfect. The program was structured at that point to enable authors to find lots of readers by utilizing Amazon's tools and programs and I was able to take advantage of it.

....

No matter how much we deny it, authors (indie or traditionally published) really are responsible for promoting our own books. When did that realization hit you?

Martin: I knew right away. I was lucky enough to have a couple wise mentors who walked me through the steps. And, my background is sales and marketing so fortunately it wasn't foreign to me.

....

You say "there are no secrets; there is simply a change in process and a change in thinking if you are going to succeed…" You look at indie publishing as a business. How important is that to being successful as a writer?

Martin: It's the difference between hopeful optimism and consistent earnings. I'm finding the longer I do this the more time I spend planning, and it's making things easier. I plan my promotions months in advance. I keep a spreadsheet that charts how I did during previous promotions. I have a list of bloggers who I work with as well as lists of promotion sites, twitter hashtags, etc. I keep those listed on www.martincrosbie.com under "Author's Tools" so that other writers can take advantage of them. And, I'm in the process of adding a list of places where you can access free photos and pictures as well as lists of places to submit your book to reviewers. It'll all be on my website in the "Author's Tools" section shortly. Although it may sound like a lot of work, once you have those lists established and the processes in place it cuts down on the time you're spending not writing.

And, the change in thinking happened for me when I realized that there were a lot of very good books that weren't being read. It isn't enough to just write a great book. That's certainly the most important element and without it nothing happens, but it's more than that. You need to approach your writing career as just that – a business where your goal is to connect with readers. That doesn't mean abandoning the muse and spending all your time formulating spreadsheets and poring over forums and blogs, balance is still very important, and writing should always come first. But, it does mean taking the time to know the industry that you're involved in and doing the things necessary to brand yourself and market your work.

....

You also believe in a "Pay it forward" policy. One of the things you wrote is, "share information, help promote others' work that you believe in, and generally help each other." How important is this philosophy to your success as an author?

Martin: I've never been involved in an industry where information, especially information that helps you connect with readers, is more freely shared. I absolutely love it. I had lots of help early in my career and I try to pay it back and forward as much as I can. Now, having said that, it doesn't always boomerang and come back to me but many times it has. I'm a believer in positive energy. I truly believe if you send out positive energy then that's what you're going to get back. That's what I try to do, and so far, it's working.

....

You use several processes to ensure your books are error free, and the best they can be. Specifically you mention using beta readers, copy editors, and proofreaders. Talk to me a little bit about beta readers. What exactly are they? How does an author go about finding beta readers? And, how can they help you improve your work?

Martin: Beta readers have quickly become an integral part of the process for writers. My first beta-readers were friends of my sister who I did now know. Now I utilize beta reader groups on Facebook or LinkedIn to find test readers for my new works. And,

I'm contacted from time to time by readers who want to help too. Beta readers are exceptional people. They take delight in finding new authors or works that they believe in. I'd be absolutely lost without them.

....

Everybody says you need an author website, and a blog. You say, "Readers are looking at places where there are books, not at author websites." I know Steve Scott says he directs most of his traffic to his Amazon Author page because that's where readers can purchase his books. You seem to agree with this strategy? How important is it to keep an up to date dynamic presence on Author Central?

Martin: One of the challenges with writing a book that helps authors succeed in self-publishing is that the world changes and in Indie world it changes quickly. When I released my self-publishing book the information in the book was absolutely current but as quickly as three months later it was already becoming dated. The basic philosophy and start-up processes remain the same but some of the marketing strategies had. So, I changed the content of the book. I updated the content and asked Amazon to alert previous purchasers that there was an updated version (which they did).

The current version, in my opinion is the most current information on the market in terms of helping authors connect with readers in a professional, cost-effective manner. There will be an even newer version updated this summer and in it I plan on talking about author websites. My thinking has changed in that regard. As an author I now want to talk about more than just my books and the process. I teach workshops, I speak at writers groups and festivals, I will soon have teaching videos available, I blog a few times a month, and as mentioned I have free lists of resources to offer authors too. I can no longer effectively do that through my Amazon Author page. There's just too much information. So, for the past few months I've had a very talented web person re-do my website. So, although your author page is very important I now believe that having a central area where you can direct your readers, one that is strictly yours, is important.

Many authors overlook print. They look at Kindle as the end all, best solution to publishing. I know in my case I couldn't make a living writing until I put my books in print using CreateSpace. Why do you think authors elect to pass over print when they publish their books?

Martin: I don't know why authors wouldn't take advantage of CreateSpace. As you know, Nick, it really doesn't cost anything to release a print book. And, there's nothing like holding a print book in your hands. Although the majority of my sales are e-books I still sell print books, especially my self-publishing guidebook.

One thing I like is that you don't look at any book as dead in the water. What is it you said, "Fortunately, you can resurrect them. You can start all over again and take another stab." I think you had to do that with your first book, **My temporary Life***, before it took off on its road to becoming a bestseller. Can you talk a little bit about how an author can breathe some new life into a seemingly dead book?*

Martin: Fortunately, the problem with **My Temporary Life** wasn't the content. I didn't have to change that. The problem was the way I was presenting the book. I had a cover that wasn't indicative of the story, a blurb that had no snap, and I wasn't utilizing Amazon's tools. When I did those things and presented my product in a more professional manner I was able to find readers. As I mentioned earlier, there are a lot of good books out there that are not being read. Sometimes all it takes is some tweaking and you can find those (sometimes) elusive readers.

You posted a blog on Indies Unlimited concerning Kindle Count Down Deals. It didn't appear that they were a great experience for you. You also talked about KDP Free Days not being what they used to be. What's your take – Free, or Count Down Deals? What's the best choice for authors?

Martin: Aha, that's the question we all want answered! Currently I am seeing results utilizing Kindle Countdown Deals through KDP

Select. I run a three day promo with my book at 99 cents and I supplement the promo with an ad on *Ereader News Today*, *Kindle Books and Tips* or *Bookbub*. As you know Nick, ENT takes 25% of your royalties from the promo day and day after, FKBT has two price levels beginning at $25, and BB pricing is in the hundreds of dollars.

From what I can determine, free giveaways don't seem to be effective right now unless you have a series of books and give away one of the books in order to experience sales of the others. I hope to be able to run a free promo again as I've had great success with them in the past. That's why I'm trying to complete the last book of my trilogy and the next book in a series that I'm writing.

....

I ran across this quote in your book, and would like your take on it. "Everything leads to something else, and you never know who might be reading your work or watching your career."

A lot of authors I've talked with, famous and not so famous, have echoed these sentiments. Some of the best things in life happen when you're not really expecting them. We talked about this earlier, with your thoughts about "Paying it forward."

....

Can you talk about a situation like this that has played out for you?

Martin: Yes, I'd love to talk about this. I have a workshop that I'm teaching this weekend and to help spread the word I've visited a lot of writers groups. I've spoken at groups where there were four or five members and some where there were packed rooms. I also blog or write articles for anyone who asks, no matter how small or large their following is. In fact I now have a tab on my website offering my services, with testimonials from some of the folks I've written for or spoken to their groups. Almost each time I've reached out and done something another opportunity has presented itself and with each opportunity I've made friends who have the ability to help me. I have friends who I count on as part of my support group and I've met them from extending my virtual hand

and asking what I can do to help. The most significant opportunity came recently. I haven't announced it yet but I will be opening the prestigious *Whistler Readers and Writers* Festival in October. I'll be teaching a one day workshop on self-publishing. It's a very progressive move for the festival and a great opportunity for me too. And, that came about because I was taking my career seriously and approaching it as a business, paying it forward and trying to help others.

About the Martin Crosbie

In a press release, Amazon called Martin Crosbie one of their success stories of 2012. His self-publishing journey has been chronicled in Publisher's Weekly, Forbes Online, and Canada's Globe and Mail newspaper. Martin's debut novel, *My Temporary Life* has been downloaded over one hundred and fifty thousand times and became an Amazon top ten overall bestseller.

He's also the author of *My Name Is Hardly* - Book Two of the *My Temporary Life Trilogy*, *Lies I Never Told* - A Collection of Short Stories, *How I Sold 30,000 eBooks on Amazon's Kindle - An Easy-To-Follow Self-Publishing Guidebook*, and *Believing Again: A Tale Of Two Christmases*.

Martin was born in the Highlands of Scotland and currently makes his home just outside Vancouver, on the west coast of Canada.

You can learn more about Martin on his new and improved *website www.martincrosbie.com*, follow him on Twitter @martinthewriter, or email him at *martin@martincrosbie.com*.

Nick Vulich

Interview with Rob Parnell

Rob Parnell

Rob Parnell has written over 40 non-fiction self-help titles and been published all over the world for the last ten years. Also a composer, singer, music producer and budding movie maker, Rob is ecstatically happy to be married to Robyn Opie Parnell, his savior and the popular bestselling children's author.

His preferred genre is the thriller - sometimes with a supernatural edge - in which he writes short stories, graphic novels, YA novels and adult thrillers.

You've been training new authors for ten years now, what's the hardest part of writing for a new author to get a handle on?

Rob: Probably the confidence to let go and allow the writing habit grab a hold of you. Too many new writers let their personality and issues get in the way of creativity. Writing should feel natural and easy, an extension of whom you are. My view is that if you're finding writing difficult, you're probably not doing it right! New authors often need to relax and stop being so hard on themselves.

....

The Writer and the Hero's Journey is a little deeper and harder to follow than most of your books. The first time I heard about Joseph Campbell's *The Hero with a Thousand Faces*, I was sitting in an American Literature class taught by David Morrell (of *Rambo* fame) at the University of Iowa back in the late seventies. It's a powerful concept to wrap your head around at first, that we all have this innate ability to understand the hero's journey. Can you give a really short run down about the hero's journey, and how it can help writers structure their stories?

Rob: Thanks for reading *The Hero's Journey* book. Currently it's the one I'm most proud of. I tried to incorporate lots of influences from writers, stories old and new and my own story as a way of 'proving' that the hero's journey concept is alive and well – and very pertinent to the writing of commercial stories. Indeed, as you imply, *Rambo* is another ideal example of the hero's journey, as is *Rocky*, of course.

Basically, the idea is that you take a normal person and thrust them into a series of increasingly difficult tests in order for him or her to gain wisdom and in the process, become a hero. Clearly this loose structure lends itself to the old idea of placing obstacles in the way of protagonists in order to provide an entertaining story. The hero's journey structure just formalizes this process – and explains why a story needs to be told this way to be truly satisfying and meaningful.

When it comes to movies especially, a hero's path and decision-making must be entirely believable. The hero's journey taps into the human condition, thereby allowing the audience to follow the hero, identify with him or her and completely relate to the character. This must happen for the story to be successful, IMHO!

....

In The Art of Story you say "we don't communicate through words…We actually communicate with our senses – in pictures, sounds, smells, and other physical reactions to stimuli – and, most importantly, with emotions." Why is that such a hard concept for new writers to understand? Can you suggest a way to naturally connect with those emotions in everyday writing?

Rob: If this is a tough concept to understand it's because we do it to ourselves. We learn to write believing that the words themselves have power and we expend a lot of energy trying to make the words work for us. But the more you write you realize the words are just the tools we use to express ideas and emotions. We need to get past the words – and really get to grips with what we're trying to describe effectively. It's a process of undoing what we're taught. I guess that's why it seems like a difficult process. The best advice is just to write more – and try not to think too hard about the words. Concentrate on feelings, images and ideas first, and then write quickly. Then edit to clarify the images and meanings rather than obscure them through literary verbosity.

....

Another concept you write about in The Art of Story is that, "To become an effective author, you'll need to be take ideas and develop them. The trick is to not write ideas down in concrete form too soon." I find most of my better ideas develop naturally when I let them fester in my brain for a while. A lot of times I'll wake up at three or four in the more, and the developed idea is there waiting for me to pound it out on the computer. Is that what you're getting a here?

Rob: Yes, it's good to wait until you feel a sense of 'completeness' and 'symmetry' to your inspiration before you commit to finalizing the idea in writing. Mainly because we tend to love what we write and don't want to mess with the words – even if the concept isn't fully developed yet.

This can lead to blocks because you don't want to screw things up and start again – even when that might be the best route to take. Developing ideas in your mind first is just about saving writing time in the long run.

....

One of the things you talk about is to illustrate story-beats with action. Could you elaborate a little more about story beats? A lot of authors talk about developing story-beats. What exactly are they, and how can authors use them to make their stories more compelling?

Rob: Ah, the big question! What each of us regards as a story beat is inherently personal. It's usually based on a feeling of what will make good plot point. If you write a series of dot points that might sum up your proposed story, for instance, each of those dot points will be a story beat. In novels especially a story beat may just be the way a protagonist feels at one particular time. In screenplays the story beat is a more formalized idea. Usually a slight emotional turning point in the text, or an event that sparks a reaction in a character, right up to the bad guy setting off a bomb or shooting someone. Story beats can be any of these things. The point of story beats is to increase empathy by manipulating emotions in the reader or viewer.

Effectively 'showing' story beats intensifies that empathy. For instance, say you have a girl who is in love with some guy. In a novel she might internalize that emotion, letting the reader know but without 'proving' it. That's passive storytelling. But when the girl touches the guy unexpectedly and says 'I love you' you're showing that beat with action and the reader feels a jolt of emotion – and empathy – because the story beat 'tugs' at the reader's own experience of being in the girl's shoes. I hope this makes sense of the issue a little. It's a complex one. If you want total overkill on the subject of story beats, I recommend you read *Story* by Robert McKee.

....

When you talk about plotting, you say "Best-selling novels tend to have very simple ideas at their heart." One example you gave was The Da Vinci Code. The premise of the story was, "What if the Catholic church was based on a lie?" Or with Harry Potter, "What if a normal school boy was secretly a wizard?" Should your plot really be that simple?

Rob: To be fair, I'm not sure many authors work this way round. Sometimes it's very hard to encapsulate our ideas into natty little sound-bites, even though it's become increasingly necessary for us to do so. I think the notion I was trying to get across is that when you have an idea that can be neatly expressed in one sentence, it's more likely the book might become a bestseller.

It's not that the premise need be simple, only that the encapsulation of it should be intriguing in as few words as possible!

....

In The Easy Way to Write Thrillers you make the point that genre dictates the way authors need to write the story. You say, "The problem with many of Sherlock Holmes' stories is that the reader is sometimes presented with solutions they could never have guessed. Nowadays that's not playing entirely fair." One thing a lot of new and experienced writers do is blur the lines between genres, or break the implied rules of their genre. How big of a problem is that?

Rob: I'm impressed that not only have you read my books but that you can quote from them so thoroughly! Sometimes it's hard to appreciate what impression your words are going to make on readers, so it's nice to know someone's taking notice. Thanks for that.

Anyway, I think blurring the lines between genres is healthy. For too long the traditional publishing industry has told us we can't do that. I don't agree. I think readers are much more savvy and flexible than they're often given credit for being. At the end of the day it's about context and what is believable. As long as the author goes out of his or her way to deal effectively with the story world in a way that doesn't threaten to undermine the reader's 'willing suspension of disbelief' then almost anything is acceptable.

Much of the time it's about not messing with the reader's expectations too much. So if you're writing a gritty urban crime thriller, then you don't want to suddenly introduce a magic time portal that enables the detective to solve the case at the end. However, if the reader knows right up front, that a detective uses his magic time portal to solve crimes then that's acceptable.

....

Another concept you talk about is character development. "Characters are the backbone of any thriller. Get them right and you're half way there." Then you suggest "archetypes are instantly recognizable character 'types' ingrained deep in our subconscious through experience, dreams, and instincts." Can you talk about this for a minute? How important are archetypes to character development? And, how can an author use archetypes to draw readers into their characters and make them more believable?

Rob: The best characters are a combination of archetype and credible personalities. Too much focus on one facet and you'll end up with something either wooden or too confusing. It's a bit like the way we deal with people in the real world. Our first instinct is to 'type' people, something we do as a survival instinct. We need to classify people quickly as either friend or foe, good or evil. Then we look deeper. We look for humanity to confirm or deny our initial impressions. Then we learn to love or hate the people we study. If you use the same process when creating fictional constructs, you should end up with believable characters.

About Rob Parnell

Rob Parnell has been writing fiction since he was five years old. Born in Winchester in the UK, he lived for a long time in London, pursuing a music career until, suitably chastised for his impertinence, moved to Adelaide, Australia, where he now teaches writing and success strategies to his many thousands of subscribers.

Visit Rob Parnell's author blog to receive weekly installments of his next super-charged thriller, The Essene Heresy. You can checkout Rob's books by visiting his *Amazon Author page*.

About the Author

N　**ick Vulich** normally writes short easy to read solutions to your ecommerce problems, but every now and then he likes to shake things up, and share his ideas on other pressing topics.

This book contains a collection of tips and tricks designed to help new, and experienced authors, navigate the maze that is self-publishing. There are so many choices available when you go to publish your book today, but there's also a boatload of conflicting advice out there. Some authors say, "Don't use Kindle Unlimited."

Others say, "KDP Free Days are useless, a thing of the past, and don't work anymore." And, still others advise, "Forget Apple, CreateSpace, audio books, and all the other self-publishing venues—the real money is on Kindle."

Who's right? Who's wrong?

Trust me. It's a hot mess out there, and it's extremely difficult to interpret and make sense out of all the conflicting advice out there.

This book is my two cents worth.

To tell you a little more about me, I've self-published my books for nearly four years now. I've sold—not, given away—nearly 75,000 copies in that time. Trust me! It hasn't made me rich, or famous. No one would mistake me, or my bank account for Stephen King, but—I've sold a shitload of books (pardon my French), and—I have a pretty decent idea which tactics work, and which ones are just a bunch of horse hockey.

I don't claim to be an expert, but I can tell you what has worked for me and hundreds of other authors.

Read the book. Feel free to try out some of my ideas. And, with just a little luck—you may see a boost in your sales.

Pay it forward, and keep writing.

October 31st, 2015
Nick Vulich
Davenport, Iowa

Books by Nick Vulich

Don't like history? You're probably reading the wrong books.

Read this book, and you're gonna think, wow! Why didn't somebody tell me that? American history is full of strange paradoxes, and that's what makes it so interesting.

The truth is much of what we learn about history is a series of little white lies that over time have grown into tall tales.

* Why doesn't everyone know the Boston Massacre wasn't really a massacre? Subsequent testimony proved the soldiers fired in self-defense. The King Street riot was started by a group of four street thugs who got their rocks off attacking lone British soldiers. Sam Adams and Paul Revere twisted it into a massacre.

* And, if you think the Boston Tea Party was a response to British taxes that raised the price of tea in the colonies, think again. The Tea Act of 1773 actually reduced the price of tea paid by the colonists. The people hurt by the Tea Act were the smugglers. The lower price of tea undercut their business, and ensured that the East India Company would have a monopoly on tea.

* The South Carolina Nullification Congress of 1832 was a harbinger of things to come. The question was if a state disagrees

with a federal law, does it have the right to nullify it, and disregard that law? Vice-president John C. Calhoun argued state's rights superseded federal laws. President Andrew Jackson believed to his dying day that Calhoun was a damned traitor, and that he should have strung him up from the nearest branch.

* The Black Hawk War was a mix-up of frontier madness, mayhem, and murder. Illinois Governor John Reynolds called out the militia and raised thousands of volunteer troops. General Winfield Scott marched his regulars half way across the country to Fort Armstrong at Rock Island. Lieutenant Colonel Zachary Taylor led a group of infantrymen in the fighting. In the end, it was a massacre that nearly wiped out the Sac tribe.

* In the fall of 1845 President Polk offered Mexico five million dollars if they would recognize the Southwestern Boundary of Texas at the Rio Grande. When Mexico refused his offer Polk decided to force the issue. He sent General Zachary Taylor and 3,000 troops to Corpus Christi, Texas. In March of 1846 General Taylor moved his forces into the disputed territory between the Rio Grande and Nueces Rivers. Soon after that, Mexico was provoked into a war with the United States.

* It has been said that James Buchanan was a "weak, timid, old man" who didn't do anything to prevent the Southern states from seceding. Some historians have even gone so far as to declare Buchanan was an "accessory after the fact." He was a president, Southern sympathizer, and traitor. But, was he?

* Imagine what it would be like to wake up, flip on the morning news, and discover Bradley Cooper or Ashton Kutcher assassinated President Obama. That's what happened in 1865. People were shocked when they learned John Wilkes Booth killed President Lincoln. Booth was one of the most popular actors of his day. He was young, just twenty-six years old, considered one of the most

attractive men in America. At the time he killed Lincoln, Booth was pulling down $20,000 a year as an actor (that's roughly $300,000 in 2015 money). And, yet—he sacrificed it all for his political beliefs. What was going on in the mind of John Wilkes Booth?

I could tell you more, but you get the idea. Things aren't always what they appear to be. There are two sides to every story. All that stuff your teacher told you in school—it may, or may not be true.

Read this book, and decide for yourself which version you should believe.

eBay 2016 is going to help you take your eBay selling to an all new level.

Section 1 looks at how to pick items that really sell on eBay. When you use the advanced search tool and these simple tips and tricks I teach you, you won't have to depend on anyone else's list to find out what's hot.

Section 2 examines email marketing and how you can use it to take your online business to an all new level. To drive the information home, I conducted an extended interview with Rob Cubbon, an expert in email marketing who gives you his take on how to approach the subject.

Section 3 is a no holds barred look at social media marketing - Facebook, Twitter, Pinterest, and more. Selling today is more about connecting with your buyers, and building lasting relationships. The days of one-and-done selling are over. Start connecting with your buyers, and watch your business grow. And, to give you that extra boost, I interviewed two sellers who are stretching the barrier with social media marketing - Lauren Lerner and Cameron Loughlin.

Section 4 discusses funding your business with Kickstarter. Crowdfunding is an all new way to fund your business, but if you aren't familiar with how it works there are a few things you need to know. The first is a Kickstarter campaign can't be used to fund an entire business. It's there to fund projects, so you need to learn how to develop your business through a series of projects. Hence, just like the old potato chip commercial, one Kickstarter is not going to be enough. Of course, I've included interviews with two people in the know on how to run a Kickstarter - Hanson Grant and Brandon Kelly.

And, by-the-way I saved the best part for last. **eBay 2016** is available in paperback now, and will be available soon as an audio book.

Order your copy today, and start building your eBay business - one step at a time.

Do you want to make more money selling on eBay?

1. Do you ever find yourself looking at successful sellers on eBay and thinking – They know something I don't.
2. They've probably got some kind of inside connection that lets them get products cheaper than I ever could.
3. They've already got the market sewed up, there's not any business left for me.

Have you ever told yourself –

1. If I had a little more money, I could buy the inventory I need to make a killing on eBay.
2. If I had a little more time, I'd be able to list enough items to be successful.
3. If I had a little more information, I could pick a killer product that would make me a million dollars selling on eBay.

Sounds crazy, doesn't it?

Every eBay book out there tells you the same thing. You need to find a great product that you can purchase at a reasonable price, and sell for a huge profit. If they don't tell you that, they tell you how easy it is to source product at garage sales, yard sales, flea markets, or the local thrift stores. And, my absolute favorite is the books that list 1001 things you can sell on eBay to make a huge profit. The only problem is half of the items they list are things you're unlikely to find – anywhere. Or, if you do a little research, you discover that fabulous selling price they told you was a one-time thing. The item is actually selling for much less now, if it is even selling at all.

Some books talk about drop shipping, or buying inventory wholesale from secret suppliers they use to make a killing selling on eBay and Amazon. Another eBay expert marketing his advice on Craigslist shows you how to source products on Amazon to sell on eBay. The secret is to discover fast selling items on Amazon, and list them for sale on eBay. When you make a sale on eBay – buy it on Amazon, and have the seller ship it to your customer. Of course, you need to purchase their entire system to make it work - $19.95 per month.

I've investigated all of these scams. And, yes – they are scams. If you buy from the majority of the "Special" wholesalers and drop shippers, you're going to discover most of the items they offer are selling on eBay for less than you paid "wholesale."

No matter what anyone tells you, selling on eBay isn't easy. It's not a sure thing. For every item that sells, another one or two items go unsold, or sell for far less than you hoped for.

eBay 2015 tells it like it is

I'm not going to tell you what to sell, where to buy it, or which items to buy. When someone guarantees you a profit they're normally feeding you a line of bull-hockey.

There's no hype, no BS, and no false promises. **eBay 2015** discusses the new eBay Seller Standards and how they affect you. It covers the problems eBay sellers encounter choosing which products to sell, how to keep accurate records, and how to ship items inexpensively and efficiently.

Learn how to –

1. Plan for success
2. Choose a niche
3. Ship like a pro
4. Sell international
5. Track your income and expenses

Selling on eBay isn't a game

You need to have a plan

eBay 2014 walks you through what it takes to sell on eBay. It answers all of your questions, and gives you ideas about how to get started and grow your eBay business.

Do you ever wonder how some sellers can grow a strong thriving business, while others barely scrape by?

Many times, I've watched two sellers as they are first starting out on eBay. Both sellers offer the exact same products and prices, yet one business skyrockets to the top of the charts selling thousands of items per month. The other business struggles to sell ten or fifteen items per month. They might even have the same basic look to their listings. On the face of it, it doesn't make sense.

Why does one eBay seller prosper, while another falls behind?

Is it a matter of luck? Does one eBay seller catch all of the breaks, while another is stuck holding doo doo? Believe it or not, many struggling sellers believe this. They think it's all a matter of luck. But, you and I know better. Don't we?

Sellers who succeed on eBay play by different rules

They don't leave anything to chance. They know that success requires a plan. You don't just move from Point A to Point B. You need to make it happen. And, that's what this book is all about. It gives you a strategy for selling on eBay.

You will learn

. How to write titles that draw buyers into your listings and help them find what you are selling
. How to take picture that show buyers what they need to know to say "This is the item I'm looking for!"
. The anatomy of a great listing. What you should say. How you should say it. What not to say.
. Why you need to stop guessing at prices for your items, and how to determine realistic prices that customers are willing to pay.
, The smart way to ship your items so you can get your packages to your customers safely and on time.
. How to rock customer service, and motivate your customers to leave five star feed-back every time.
. How to deal with eBay's constant string of updates and changes

Still not convinced?

Consider this.

. There are over 149 million active buyers on eBay.
. Last year they spent over $83 billion dollars on everything from paperclips to new cars and custom helicopters.

. Hundreds of thousands of small sellers are making $500, a $1000, even $2500 every month working part time from their kitchen table or garage.

How about you?

Are you making your fair share?

If not, this book will help you understand - selling on eBay isn't a game. You need to have a plan.

. **Get serious about your eBay selling**
. **Order this book - TODAY!**
. **Make more sales tomorrow - and everyday**

www.ingramcontent.com/pod-product-compliance
Lightning Source LLC
Chambersburg PA
CBHW020909180526
45163CB00007B/2677